BELIEF IN MARRIAGE

The Evidence for Reforming Weddings Law

Rebecca Probert, Rajnaara C. Akhtar,
and Sharon Blake

BRISTOL
UNIVERSITY
PRESS

First published in Great Britain in 2023 by

Bristol University Press
University of Bristol
1–9 Old Park Hill
Bristol
BS2 8BB
UK
t: +44 (0)117 374 6645
e: bup-info@bristol.ac.uk

Details of international sales and distribution partners are available at bristoluniversitypress.co.uk

British Library Cataloguing in Publication Data
A catalogue record for this book is available from the British Library

ISBN 978-1-5292-3047-5 paperback
ISBN 978-1-5292-3048-2 ePub
ISBN 978-1-5292-3049-9 ePdf

Cover design: Liam Roberts Design
Front cover image: Unsplash/@andknech

To all the couples who were unable to marry in accordance with their beliefs, in the hope that that their stories will pave the way for law reform

Contents

Acknowledgements

The research that underpins this book was conducted while the Law Commission was carrying out its project on weddings law reform. It was designed to provide the Law Commission with valuable information about the way that weddings law operates in practice. During this time, Rebecca Probert was also the specialist advisor to the Law Commission. However, the analysis underpinning this book was a collaborative effort between all three authors, with Rajnaara C. Akhtar and Sharon Blake being entirely independent of the Law Commission.

The research was conducted under the difficult circumstances collectively faced by us all during the COVID-19 pandemic. The research team is extremely grateful to a wide range of people who made the research possible despite the restrictions in place while conducting fieldwork.

The research was funded by the Nuffield Foundation, and Ash Patel, Christopher Milton, and Ellen Wright provided guidance, support, and advice throughout the project. Dr Vishal Vora, a co-investigator during part of the project, took the lead on data collection from Hindu and Sikh communities, and Dr Tania Barton performed a vital role as research coordinator during the fieldwork stages of the project. Our advisory group – Anne Barber (Director, Civil Ceremonies Ltd), Frank Cranmer (Honorary Research Fellow, Centre for Law and Religion, Cardiff University; Fellow, St Chad's College, Durham), Siddique Patel (Deputy Director, Register Our Marriage; Partner, Gunnercooke LLP), Professor Nawal Prinja (Vishwa Hindu Parishad), Teddy Prout (formerly Director of Community Services, Humanists UK), Nazia Rashid (Muslim Council of Britain; family law solicitor and mediator, Anthony Gold), Professor Liz Trinder (University of Exeter), and Dr Islam Uddin (imam and academic researcher) – helped with the recruitment of participants and provided feedback on both our report and our separate briefing paper to the Law Commission. We used several avenues to recruitment and are also grateful to the many organizations and individuals across England and Wales who supported these efforts. At our respective universities, Lucy Gregson-Green, David Naylor, Afzal Ghumra, Lyndsay Kirby, Laura Kempin, Dave Walsh, Tim Hillier, Jo Richardson, and Aamir Hussain (De Montfort University), Kate Gannon and Mandy

Schuster (University of Exeter), and Jennifer Paterson, Annette Hayden, Debbie Bloxham, and Ana Aliverti (University of Warwick) all provided valuable support on different aspects of the project.

We would also like to thank Rebecca Munday, a PhD candidate at the University of Exeter, for sharing her dissertation on Pagan weddings with the team, and Liam Brown for additional research and proofreading.

Finally, this project would not have been possible without all the participants who shared their views, opinions, and wedding experiences with us, and we reserve our most profound gratitude for them. It is always a privilege for us as researchers to hear personal stories and share key moments from our participants' lives. Along with the joyful and happy memories, we also spoke to participants who had difficult experiences. We are grateful to them all for giving us their time, each adding to the layers of richness in this research.

Introduction

It was an idyllic summer's day. The sun shone on the weathered stone of the old house and the tiny Anglican parish church that stood on the other side of its garden. The bride's white lace gown swished softly over the grass as she and her father walked down the aisle between the benches where the guests were seated to where the groom was waiting by an archway covered with roses. An imam presided over their exchange of vows and gave a sermon explaining the commonalities between Islam and other faiths. Everyone then proceeded to the church, where the legally recognized wedding was led by an Anglican clergyman. No hymns were sung, on account of the COVID-19 restrictions then in place, but the bride's mother read a passage from the Koran. The couple then proceeded back to the garden, where the groom's mother read a passage from the Bible and the couple signed a *nikah* contract.

Beautiful though the ceremonies were, it was not quite what the couple had wanted. Their original wish had been to have a single ceremony that reflected their respective beliefs and was jointly led by this imam and a Christian pastor who had known the groom since childhood. As the bride put it, having a combined ceremony "was, if anything, the most important thing in our wedding ... to subtly reinforce the fact that someone who is Muslim and someone who is Christian *could* get married".[1] They had then discovered that to have a legally recognized wedding at their first choice of venue, the ceremony would have to be conducted by registration officers and could not include any religious content. While they could have legally married at a register office before or after having a religious ceremony, this was unattractive to them as they wanted the moment they became married

---

[1] This was not a general concern about how a marriage between two people of different faiths might be seen, but a specific allusion to the differences of opinion that exist in Islamic jurisprudence on whether a Muslim woman can marry a non-Muslim man. See further Chapter 5, which also discusses why it was not possible for the *nikah* ceremony to be held in the church.

both religiously and legally to be shared with family and friends at the same place and time. As the nearest mosque that was registered for weddings was over 50 miles away, having their legal wedding in the Church of England and a separate *nikah* was the only option left.

Their case – one of over 80 that we explored as part of an empirical research project – provides a powerful example of the complexity and constraints of the current laws governing weddings and how couples may not be able to marry in the form and ceremony of their choosing. It is those constraints and choices, and how they intersect with religious or other beliefs, that are the focus of this book.

In this introductory chapter, we first explain our aims in writing this book and its significance both to current policy debates and to broader global debates about the regulation of marriage. We then provide some context about weddings and beliefs (both religious and non-religious) in England and Wales today to show why we think that the topic of belief in marriage is an important one despite the apparent decline in the number of religious weddings recorded as having taken place in the two countries. After describing the evidence that underpins our analysis, we set out an overview of the chapters that follow.

Aims

In exploring the role of belief in marriage,[2] we have two key aims: first, to assess how far the current law in England and Wales enables couples to legally marry in line with their beliefs and, second, to show why the law *should* enable couples to have a legally recognized wedding in line with their beliefs.

Throughout the book, references to 'beliefs' encompass non-religious belief systems such as Humanism as well as religious beliefs (unless otherwise stated), and the terms 'legally marry' and 'legally recognized wedding' are used to distinguish what the law recognizes as a valid marriage from what many couples in the study saw as their 'real' wedding.[3] We should also note that

---

[2] Our focus is specifically on marriage; civil partnerships operate differently in that it is signing the relevant documentation that creates a civil partnership, rather than what is said during the ceremony. The signing may be accompanied by a religious ceremony, but that is a different matter. We think it is important that this option should remain: couples who do not believe in marriage should have the option of formalising their relationship in a way that is not modelled on a marriage ceremony. However, the fact that the civil partnership is entirely a statutory creation and has no counterpart within any religion or belief system means that it falls outside the scope of this book.

[3] The question of when a marriage will be recognized as valid is not entirely straightforward as it depends not only on the degree of compliance with the legal requirements but also on whether any failures to comply were 'knowing and wilful'. A marriage will be void if the parties 'knowingly and wilfully' (Marriage Act 1949, ss 25 and 49) failed to

our focus is primarily on the ceremony rather than on all of the steps that are required for a legally recognized wedding; we recognize, for example, that the state has an interest in requiring couples to give notice in advance of the wedding so that checks as to their identity and capacity can be made and any impediments to the marriage identified, and we are not seeking to argue that such safeguards should be dispensed with.[4] As we will discuss, we think that the criteria for the ceremony should be aligned more closely with what couples believe constitutes their marriage, in line with the Law Commission's recommendations for reform.[5]

In relation to our first key aim, it might appear that the law does already make provision for couples to marry in accordance with their beliefs. While the relevant legislation, the Marriage Act 1949, only makes specific mention of Church of England, Quaker, and Jewish weddings, in principle any other religious group may register its place of worship for weddings.[6] The relevant provisions have been described as providing 'a gateway for the legal recognition of marriages that adopt the form and ceremony of other religions'.[7] And for these purposes, the concept of what constitutes a religion is a broad one that need not involve a belief in any specific deity, simply a belief that 'there is more to be understood about mankind's nature and relationship to the universe than can be gained from the senses or from science'.[8]

Yet while the law's concept of what constitutes a religion is broad, non-religious belief organizations do not have the option of registering their meeting places for weddings and so are not able to conduct legally binding weddings.[9] Moreover, being able to get married in a particular place of worship is not necessarily the same as being able to marry in accordance

---

comply with certain key provisions. A ceremony may also be classified as 'non-qualifying' (*AG v Akhter and Khan* [2020] EWCA Civ 122) if the parties married outside the legal framework altogether. For a more detailed explanation of these distinctions and their consequences, see Rebecca Probert, Rajnaara C. Akhtar, and Sharon Blake (2022) *When Is a Wedding Not a Marriage? Exploring Non-legally Binding Marriage Ceremonies: Final Report* (Nuffield Foundation), ch 3.

4   The detailed requirements governing the preliminaries are set out in Law Commission (2020) *Getting Married: A Consultation Paper on Weddings Law* (3 September), ch 2.

5   Law Commission (2022) *Celebrating Marriage: A New Weddings Law* (19 July).

6   Marriage Act 1949, s 41. See further Chapters 3 and 4.

7   *R (ota Harrison) v Secretary of State for Justice* [2020] EWHC 2096 (Admin), [9], per Eady J.

8   *R (Hodkin) v Registrar General of Births, Deaths and Marriages* [2013] UKSC 77, [57], per Lord Toulson.

9   All-Party Parliamentary Humanist Group (2018) *'Any Lawful Impediment?' A Report of the All-Party Parliamentary Humanist Group's Inquiry into the Legal Recognition of Humanist Marriage in England and Wales*: https://humanists.uk/wp-content/uploads/APPHG-rep ort-on-humanist-marriage.pdf

with one's beliefs. A wedding in a registered place of worship can take place according to the form and ceremony of the couple's choosing but has to include certain prescribed words and be conducted in the presence of a person authorized to complete the paperwork.[10] As we will show, these apparently neutral requirements enable Christians to believe that their religious weddings are legally recognized[11] and lead non-Christians to believe that their religious weddings are legally irrelevant.[12] As a result, those whose legally recognized wedding took place in a mosque, temple, or gurdwara did not necessarily see themselves as having legally married in accordance with their beliefs, but regarded themselves as having had a civil wedding in addition to their religious ceremony.

This disjunction between what is legally possible and how that law is experienced explains why one person can write that 'it is today possible to marry in a Hindu or Sikh temple [or] in a Mosque'[13] and another that Hindu, Sikh, and Muslim marriages 'are not recognised under the law'.[14] Both are right, because each is making a slightly different claim: the option of getting married in a Hindu temple does not mean that the Hindu marriage ceremony is recognized.[15]

For present purposes, the crucial question is whether couples *believed* themselves to have married in accordance with their beliefs. In order to answer this, in the chapters that follow we provide a contextual analysis of the legislative framework in England and Wales to ascertain what is possible, what is practicable, and how the law is perceived.

In showing why the law *should* enable couples to marry in line with their beliefs, we are not suggesting that the question of what constitutes a legal marriage should simply be delegated to religious groups to decide.[16] The case law on the application of religious law to questions of validity shows

---

[10] Marriage Act 1949, s 44.

[11] See Chapter 3.

[12] See Chapter 4.

[13] Stephen Cretney (2007) 'Relationships: law, content and form' in Carola Thorpe and Judith Trowell (eds) *Re-rooted Lives: Inter-disciplinary Work within the Family Justice System* (Jordans), 163.

[14] Shaista Gohir (2016) *Information and Guidance on Muslim Marriage and Divorce in Britain* (Muslim Women's Network UK), 27.

[15] The question of what it means for a particular type of wedding to be 'recognized' is a particularly complex one. From one perspective, only Anglican weddings are recognized in and of themselves, while the legal recognition of other weddings, including Quaker or Jewish ones, depends on compliance with additional legal requirements. See further Chapter 2.

[16] For discussion of the issues this may entail, see Joel A. Nichols (ed) (2012) *Marriage and Divorce in a Multicultural Context: Multi-tiered Marriage and the Boundaries of Civil Law and Religion* (Cambridge University Press).

that this approach does not necessarily result in a ceremony being upheld.[17] Our starting assumption is therefore that there will continue to be a statutory framework setting out the requirements for a legally recognized wedding, but that this framework could and should be revised to ensure that it operates equally for all beliefs.

In thinking about the role of belief within the legal framework, we take up the question posed by Jane Mair in her perceptive article on belief in marriage, which inspired the title of our book. She asked: 'Is religious marriage simply a remnant of earlier times, has it become a consumer-friendly system which allows religious couples to satisfy legal and faith commitments in one cost-effective ceremony or might it be an important aspect of the expressive function of family law?'[18] Our findings suggest that 'belief weddings' – that is, a wedding that reflects either religious or non-religious beliefs[19] – do, or could, perform an important expressive function. First, rules that give those of different beliefs the same opportunity to marry in accordance with their beliefs send an important message about respect, equality, and inclusion. Second, being able to get married in a way that reflects one's beliefs affects the nature of the process and gives additional weight and meaning to it.[20] As John Eekelaar has commented:

> Most people see marriage as a major event in their personal lives, which for many can only be adequately expressed if it has been brought about in a manner in accordance with a deeply held belief, or in a way that holds strong meaning for them. The logical (if radical) outcome of recognising this is that it should not matter what type of ceremony accompanies the formation of the marriage if it fulfils those requirements for the parties.[21]

These are issues to which we will return. We turn now to consider the significance of these particular issues.

Significance

The research that underpins this book was carried out at the same time the Law Commission was conducting a review of the law governing weddings. As the Law Commission explained in a consultation paper

---

[17] See further Chapter 2.
[18] Jane Mair (2015) 'Belief in marriage' 5 *International Journal of the Jurisprudence of the Family* 63, 84.
[19] Law Commission (2022), para 2.3.
[20] See further Chapter 10.
[21] John Eekelaar (2013) 'Marriage: a modest proposal' 43 *Family Law* 83, 85.

published in 2020, the terms of reference of this review were 'to provide recommendations for a reformed law of weddings that allows for greater choice within a simple, fair, and consistent legal structure'.[22] Having identified how the differential treatment of different beliefs within the current law meant that some couples had 'more freedom to have a ceremony that is meaningful to them than others', it recommended a new scheme that would 'assist couples and religious organisations for whom the current law simply does not work'.[23]

Under this new scheme, the differences between different religious groups would be reduced, if not removed entirely.[24] Registering a building would no longer be the 'gateway' for conducting legal weddings: all religious groups that meet certain criteria would be able to nominate officiants to oversee weddings.[25] Those weddings would not need to include any words prescribed by law: the moment at which a couple become married in the eyes of the law would be the moment at which they become married in the eyes of their religion, whether that entails certain words being said or certain actions being performed.[26] In this way, all religious groups would be able to conduct weddings in much the same way that the Society of Friends and various Jewish groups have been able to since 1837. At the same time, the legal restrictions that currently apply only to Quaker and Jewish weddings would be removed.[27] In addition, depending on decisions taken by the government,[28] non-religious belief organizations would be able to nominate officiants on the same basis as religious organizations, and civil weddings could be officiated by independent officiants as well as by registration officers.

---

[22] Law Commission (2020), para 1.68.

[23] Law Commission (2022), para 2.9.

[24] Anglican weddings would still stand on a slightly different footing in that Anglican preliminaries would still be recognized as legal preliminaries and clergy authorized to exercise ordained ministry within the Church of England or Church in Wales would automatically be recognized as officiants: see Law Commission (2022), paras 3.23 and 4.105.

[25] Law Commission (2022), para 4.256. The criteria are that '(1) the organisation has been established for a minimum period, during which period it has had members from at least 20 households who meet regularly in person for worship or in furtherance of or to practise their beliefs; ... (2) it has a policy about nominating and monitoring officiants; and (3) it would be a manifestation of an individual's religion or beliefs to have a wedding officiated at by an officiant nominated by that organisation'.

[26] Law Commission (2022), para 5.78.

[27] See further Chapter 2.

[28] The Law Commission's terms of reference were to devise a scheme that could include non-religious belief organizations and independent celebrants, but the decision as to whether the scheme *should* include them rests with the government: Law Commission (2022), para 1.49.

The negative perceptions that many of the study participants had of the current law contrasted sharply with their positive assessment of the Law Commission's proposals for reform.[29] The implementation of its recommendations would enable far more couples to have a legal wedding that reflects their beliefs, and the pages that follow provide further evidence of the importance of this.

While our focus is on the law of England and Wales, our findings also have relevance for the way in which entry into marriage is regulated in other countries. Across the globe, the majority of jurisdictions make provision for couples to enter into a legally recognized marriage via religious rites.[30] But that does not necessarily mean that all religious groups stand on the same footing. In any jurisdiction where entry into marriage was originally governed by a national church or single religious grouping, the law is likely to bear the imprint of the past, whether in only recognizing certain religious groups as able to conduct weddings or, more subtly, in apparently neutral rules about the formalities that are required.[31] Such rules may not only reflect particular religious values but also, on a practical level, be easier for some groups to satisfy than others. Empirical research has established how Muslim couples in different European jurisdictions have experienced similar issues in navigating the legal requirements for a valid marriage.[32]

Our findings also have relevance for those jurisdictions that have universal civil marriage.[33] While our participants' comments on the impact of

---

[29] See Rebecca Probert, Rajnaara C. Akhtar and Sharon Blake, *When Is a Wedding not a Marriage? Exploring Non-legally Binding Marriage Ceremonies: A Briefing Paper for the Law Commission* (2021), and see further Chapter 10.

[30] This is the case not only within other common law jurisdictions such as Australia, Canada, New Zealand, and South Africa, but also across Europe, with legally recognized religious weddings being an option in Croatia, the Republic of Cyprus, the Czech Republic, Denmark, Estonia, Finland, Greece, Italy, Latvia, Lithuania, Malta, Portugal, Slovakia, Spain, and Sweden. Most African and Asian countries also make provision for religious weddings, China and North Korea being notable exceptions.

[31] See, for example, Caroline Sörgjerd (2012) *Reconstructing Marriage: The Legal Status of Relationships in a Changing Society* (Intersentia), 204, which discussed the position in Sweden.

[32] See, for example, Federica Sona (2018) '"Mosque marriages" and nuptial forms among Muslims in Italy' 7 *Oxford Journal of Law and Religion* 519; Anja Bredal (2018) 'Contesting the boundaries between civil and religious marriage: state and mosque discourse in pluralistic Norway' 6 *Sociology of Islam* 297; Ibtisam Sadegh and David E. Zamiit (2018) 'Legitimizing a Muslim marriage in Malta: navigating legal and normative structures' 7 *Oxford Journal of Law and Religion* 498.

[33] Such jurisdictions are, it should be noted, a minority in global terms: see Rebecca Probert (forthcoming 2024) 'Universal civil marriage: a blueprint for the future or an idea whose time has passed?' in Rebecca Probert and Sharon Thompson (eds) *Research Handbook on Marriage, Cohabitation and the Law* (Edward Elgar). In broad terms, jurisdictions have

separating the legal wedding from the more meaningful ceremony cannot simply be transposed to such jurisdictions – after all, it may be that the resentment at having to have a separate legal wedding is lessened when this is required of all couples – they do raise questions as to how universal civil marriage is perceived and experienced.[34] Seen as a strategy adopted in earlier centuries as part of the shift in the balance of power from church to state or to underline the unity or modernity of a new nation-state,[35] universal civil marriage may have served its purpose. Increased secularization means that recognizing religious forms of marriage would pose no challenge to the authority of the state; this recognition might also be more successful than universal civil marriage in integrating communities who regard the religious rite as more important than the legal wedding.[36]

Indeed, in recent decades the global trend has been towards extending, rather than restricting, the ways in which couples can marry. Scotland, Northern Ireland, and the Republic of Ireland all now make provision for non-religious belief weddings as well as religious ones.[37] Independent celebrants have been able to conduct weddings in Australia and New Zealand since the 1970s, and recent reforms in Guernsey and Jersey make provision for celebrants to be authorized to conduct weddings there.[38] The question as to the role to be accorded to different kinds of beliefs in devising the rules for entry into marriage is therefore one that arises whether religiosity is declining, diversifying, or intensifying.

Context

On 19 May 2022, the Office for National Statistics released the official statistics on marriage in England and Wales for the year 2019.[39] Its headline figures were couched in rather negative terms: there had been a 6.4 per

---

tended to introduce universal civil marriage as a demonstration of the power of the state, often as a reaction against the Catholic Church or as part of communist ideology.

[34] See, for example, Maaike Voorhoeve (2018) 'Law and social change in Tunisia: the case of unregistered marriage' 7 *Oxford Journal of Law and Religion* 479, for an exploration of the conflict between social norms and the laws imposed by an authoritarian state.

[35] On which see Rebecca Probert (2020) 'State and law' in Paul Puschmann (ed) *A Cultural History of Marriage in the Age of Empires* (Bloomsbury).

[36] For discussion of religious-only marriages in jurisdictions that have universal civil marriage, see, for example, Annalies Moors, Martijn de Koning, and Vanessa Vroon-Najem (2018) 'Secular rule and Islamic ethics: engaging with Muslim-only marriages in the Netherlands' 6 *Sociology of Islam* 274.

[37] See Chapter 7.

[38] Marriage (Bailiwick of Guernsey) Law 2020; Marriage and Civil Status (Jersey) Law 2001, as amended by the Marriage and Civil Status (Jersey) Order 2018.

[39] Office for National Statistics (2022) 'Marriages in England and Wales: 2019' (19 May).

cent decline in weddings overall compared to 2018, with the number of opposite- and same-sex weddings alike going down; and at 18.7 per cent, fewer than one in five opposite-sex couples had a religious wedding, the lowest percentage on record, while only 0.7 per cent of same-sex weddings had been religious ones.

The figures prompted a few jeremiads in the media about the decline of marriage,[40] with a number of commentators highlighting the particularly sharp decline in the number of religious weddings.[41] Yet the fact that 439,700 individuals chose to enter into a legally recognized marriage in England and Wales[42] in 2019 despite the removal of many of the incentives to marry[43] does indicate that marriage is still statistically and socially important.

Moreover, when we drill down into the different types of legally recognized religious weddings that are taking place, it is clear that the statistics do not tell the whole story about how couples might wish to marry. People in some religious groups are far more likely to marry in a religious wedding than people in others. In 2019, 72.4 per cent of religious weddings were Anglican, 10.1 per cent were Catholic, 12 per cent were conducted according to the rites of other Christian groups, and 5.4 per cent were conducted in non-Christian places of worship.[44] While Christians still outnumber followers of other faiths in England and Wales, they are not 20 times as numerous. To put it another way, just 2,143 legally recognized weddings in registered places of worship were recorded for approximately 3.9 million Muslims, 1 million Hindus, 524,000 Sikhs, 273,000 Buddhists, and 348,000 followers of other religions.[45]

---

[40] See, for example, *Mail Online* (2022) 'Number of marriages slumps to lowest level since Queen Victoria was on the throne', 19 May; Melanie McDonagh (2022) 'Our carelessness towards marriage will cost us dear', *The Times*, 23 May.

[41] See, for example, the *Independent Online* (2022), 'Marriage rates for opposite-sex couples drop to new record low', 19 May, emphasizing the 'long-term fall in the proportion of marriages that are religious ceremonies', and *The Times* (2022), 'Marriage rate drops to lowest on record', 20 May, noting that there had been 'a 60.4 per cent decrease in opposite-sex religious ceremonies over the past two decades'.

[42] It should be noted that the figures only record weddings that took place in England and Wales, not the number of people resident in England and Wales who got married. On the basis of data from the International Passenger Survey, it can be tentatively suggested that 63,900 individuals usually resident in England or Wales travelled overseas to get married in 2019, while 3,500 overseas residents married in England or Wales: see Office for National Statistics (2022) 'Marriages' and (2008) 'Report: marriages abroad 2002–2007' 133 *Population Trends* 65.

[43] On which see Rebecca Probert (2012) *The Changing Legal Regulation of Cohabitation: From Fornicators to Family, 1600–2010* (Cambridge University Press).

[44] Office for National Statistics (2022) 'Marriages'.

[45] Office for National Statistics (2022) 'Religion, England and Wales: Census 2021' (29 November).

The disjunction between the number of religious weddings of different types and the religious profile of England and Wales suggests that more attention needs to be paid to what is practicable, as well as what is possible, in interpreting the statistics on how couples marry. It should also be remembered that the official statistics, by definition, only record legal weddings. While the precise number of religious-only marriages is unknown, and the reasons for entering into such a marriage are complex,[46] our data suggests many couples have a belief ceremony in addition to the civil wedding which is recorded and that more couples would enter into a legal marriage if they could do so in a way that reflected their beliefs.[47]

In assessing the relationship between religious beliefs and religious weddings, it should be noted that the decisive shift away from religious weddings only occurred in the late 1990s, when it became possible to have a civil wedding on approved premises such as hotels and stately homes.[48] Having a greater choice of attractive venues undoubtedly meant that many couples who might previously have chosen to marry in a place of worship for its aesthetic qualities, despite having no religious beliefs, were able to marry in a way that reflected their lack of beliefs. But there are also many couples who marry on approved premises and have a separate religious ceremony to reflect their beliefs.

To the many couples who have a religious marriage ceremony before or after a legally recognized wedding should also be added the increasing number choosing to have a ceremony led by a Humanist celebrant. In *R (ota Harrison) v Secretary of State for Justice*, in which the High Court considered a complaint by six Humanist couples that the current law breached their rights under the European Convention on Human Rights, the court heard evidence from Humanists UK that it had 260 celebrants conducting around 1,000 ceremonies in England and Wales each year.[49] In addition, as we will show, ceremonies conducted by independent celebrants or, on a more informal basis, by a friend or relative of the couple may also reflect the beliefs of the parties.

These additional ceremonies expose the extent to which the legal options for getting married do not reflect how couples actually want to be married.

---

[46] On which see Rajnaara C. Akhtar, Patrick Nash, and Rebecca Probert (eds) (2020) *Cohabitation and Religious Marriage: Status, Similarities and Solutions* (Bristol University Press).

[47] See further Chapter 9.

[48] For analysis of this shift, see John Haskey (1998) 'Marriages in "approved premises" in England and Wales: the impact of the 1994 Marriage Act' 93 *Population Trends* 38; John Walliss (2002) '"Loved the wedding, invite me to the marriage": the secularisation of weddings in contemporary Britain' 7 *Sociological Research Online*: https://doi.org/10.5153/sro.765

[49] [2020] EWHC 2096 (Admin), [27].

As we will show, many couples who are formally recorded as marrying in a civil wedding do not regard that as their 'real' wedding.

Our evidence

To show how the law is experienced in practice, we will draw on data from our project on non-legally binding wedding ceremonies. This project, funded by the Nuffield Foundation, was a qualitative research study into non-legally binding wedding ceremonies in England and Wales. It set out to explore the reasons people have for going through non-legally binding wedding ceremonies and the role of those who conduct them. We spoke to 170 individuals who either had had at least one non-legally binding ceremony or had been involved in conducting such ceremonies.[50] Unlike much of the existing literature, which has focused on religious-only marriages within Muslim communities, our project also examined ceremonies that took place in *addition* to a legal wedding. These included Bahá'í, Buddhist, Christian, Hindu, Humanist, interfaith, Jewish, Pagan, Sikh, and Zoroastrian ceremonies as well as ones led by independent celebrants.

There was a range of reasons why those we interviewed had two separate ceremonies, which we analyzed in our report.[51] Our focus here is on how they described their beliefs, how their ceremony – if not necessarily their legally recognized wedding – aligned with those beliefs, and how they would have welcomed the option of getting legally married in a way that reflected those beliefs.

We should note that the only criterion for inclusion in our study was that the individual had had a *non*-legally binding ceremony or had conducted one. As a result, the study focused on individuals for whom the current law does not cater, and it cannot be taken as representative of all couples getting married in England and Wales.[52] Nonetheless, it provides important insights

---

[50] For those who had a non-legally binding ceremony, we used the semi-structured interview method, generally interviewing one member of the couple who had married (except for five interviews with both members of the couples). Where we refer to 'interviewees' in the book, it is this group to which we are referring. For those involved in conducting ceremonies, we primarily used focus groups. However, group interviews (generally with two participants) and individual interviews were also used, both for convenience in terms of scheduling and to enable individuals to speak more freely than they might otherwise have done.

[51] See Rebecca Probert, Rajnaara C. Akhtar, and Sharon Blake (2022).

[52] For a full explanation of the composition of our sample, see Chapter 2 of our report. For the purposes of this book, participants have been given pseudonyms (see Appendix). All of the data has been anonymized, and details that might lead to the identification of particular individuals have been removed.

into perceptions of the legal constraints as well as how individuals' experiences of the process of getting married differed depending on their beliefs.

The structure of the book

Chapters 2 through to 8 each look at a different set of beliefs or type of ceremony, with the sequence reflecting the extent to which those beliefs are accommodated by the existing law. In each of these chapters, we provide a description of the ceremonies being discussed to illustrate the different forms that weddings take within different traditions. Even within our sample, however, wedding ceremonies varied widely depending on numerous factors, including ethnicity, age, and whether either party had been married before, not to mention cost. We do not seek to provide a comprehensive overview of every ceremony but hope that these descriptions aid understanding.

We therefore begin with the special treatment accorded to Anglican, Quaker, and Jewish weddings: as Chapter 2 will show, only Anglican weddings provide a purely religious route to a legal wedding, and the privileges accorded to Quaker and Jewish weddings may be more evident at an organizational level than an individual one.

Chapters 3 and 4 examine weddings in registered places of worship, with Chapter 3 explaining how the option was designed for Christian weddings and how the legal requirements operate in practice to encourage a sense that the law recognizes Christian weddings, and Chapter 4 showing how the converse applies to non-Christian weddings in registered places of worship, with identical legal requirements intersecting with religious rites in a very different way. Those differences in practice are also central to Chapter 5, which explores the particular challenges that arise where couples are of different faiths or where only one person in the couple holds religious or other beliefs.

In Chapters 6, 7, 8, and 9, we turn to consider the types of ceremonies for which the law makes no real provision at present. Pagan weddings, considered in Chapter 6, merit separate consideration, largely because most Pagan places of worship are not buildings at all and so do not qualify to be registered under the current law. Chapter 7 turns to the issue of belief in Humanist ceremonies, Chapter 8 considers the extent to which ceremonies led by independent celebrants may also be used to reflect a couple's beliefs, and Chapter 9 explores how having a ceremony led by a friend or family member may be important for a couple to marry in accordance with their beliefs.

In each of these chapters, we discuss the implications of the Law Commission's recommendations for reform for the type of ceremony in question. Chapter 10 returns to the broader question of why we think the law *should* enable couples to marry in line with their beliefs.

2

Anglican, Quaker, and Jewish Weddings

'We already have some of those freedoms, and I don't see why we should be allowed to have them and nobody else is allowed to have them.'[1]

Introduction

In this chapter, we analyze the three types of religious wedding that are explicitly mentioned in the Marriage Act 1949 – those conducted according to Anglican[2] rites and those conducted according to Quaker or Jewish usages.

The rules that apply to these groups are different from those that apply to other religious groups. As we will discuss in more detail in the chapters that follow, weddings in the registered places of worship of all other religious groups, including Christian ones, must be preceded by civil preliminaries, include words prescribed by statute, and take place in the presence of either an authorized person or civil registrar.[3] Anglican weddings, by contrast, may be preceded by their own preliminaries and conducted by a member of the clergy according to their own liturgy. Similarly, although Quaker and Jewish weddings must be preceded by civil preliminaries, they can take

---

[1]   Rachael, a rabbi, commenting on the Law Commission's proposals for reform.
[2]   Throughout the chapter, we use the term 'Anglican' to refer both to the established Church of England and to the disestablished Church in Wales. The relevant law applicable to both is set out in Part II of the Marriage Act 1949 (although see Sch 6 for a list of the provisions that do not apply to the Church in Wales). Where we refer to the Church of England alone, this is either because we are discussing the position before the creation of a separate Church in Wales (by virtue of the Welsh Church Act 1914) or because the point we are making applies only to the Church of England.
[3]   See further Chapters 3 and 4.

13

place anywhere, according to their own usages, and the person responsible for their registration need not even be in attendance.[4]

For these three groups, then, the answer to our overarching question of whether the current law enables couples to marry in line with their beliefs would appear to be a simple yes. Yet as we shall show, formal recognition of specific rites and usages brings its own constraints. We look first at Anglican weddings, explaining how the current legislative framework originated in the Church's own rules and showing how the established nature of the Church of England limits its freedom to decide who it can marry (and how). We then turn to Quaker and Jewish weddings, tracing their history to show why they have a special status under the Marriage Act 1949 and showing how they are less free from regulation than they might at first appear. As part of this discussion, we will set out the key elements of Anglican, Quaker, and Jewish ceremonies in order to show that the recognition accorded to these particular religious rites does not depend on the nature of those rites.

Anglican weddings

Legislating for Anglican weddings

From its establishment in the 16th century to the mid–18th century,[5] the canon law of the Church of England determined how couples could marry. It directed that weddings should take place in the local church of the parties after banns had been called or, exceptionally, a licence had been granted.[6] Whether a marriage was valid – a question that fell to the Church courts to determine – depended on whether it had been solemnized by an Anglican clergyman rather than on whether all of the canonical requirements had been observed.

The Clandestine Marriages Act 1753 marked the beginning of the shift from regulation by the church to regulation by the state. Legislating for Anglican marriage made it clear that it was the state that was the ultimate

---

[4] For discussion of the legal rules applicable to Anglican, Quaker, and Jewish weddings, see Law Commission (2020) *Getting Married: A Consultation Paper on Weddings Law* (3 September), paras 2.64–2.137.

[5] With the exception of a brief interlude under the Commonwealth in the mid–17th century when couples had to marry before magistrates: An Act touching Marriages and the registering thereof; and also touching Births and Burials 1653. For discussion, see Christopher Durston (1988) '"Unhallowed wedlocks": the regulation of marriage during the English revolution' 31 *Historical Journal* 45.

[6] For a more detailed discussion of the requirements of the canon law, see Rebecca Probert (2009) *Marriage Law and Practice in the Long Eighteenth Century: A Reassessment* (Cambridge University Press).

arbiter and guarantor of validity.[7] For present purposes, however, the key point is that the 1753 Act simply gave effect to the requirements of the canon law. Neither it nor its replacement in the form of the Marriage Act 1823 fundamentally changed the substance of what was required for an Anglican wedding. Similarly, when the Marriage Act 1836 ended the Church of England's virtual monopoly over weddings,[8] it made little change to the framework governing Anglican weddings.[9]

Disestablishment did not affect this framework either. The Church in Wales, which formally came into being in 1920, retained the same powers to conduct weddings as the Church of England, insofar as banns and licences continued to be legal preliminaries to such weddings, Welsh churches and chapels did not need to be registered for weddings, and Welsh clergy were still able to conduct weddings by virtue of their office.[10] While canon law ceased to exist as law in Wales,[11] weddings continued to be one of the 'vestiges of establishment'.[12]

With the Marriage Act 1949 being merely a consolidating measure, the fundamentals of the legal framework within which Anglican weddings take place are still those of the pre-1753 canon law. Today, Anglican weddings can still provide a purely religious route to a legal wedding, in that they alone may be preceded by their own preliminaries and conducted by their own clergy according to their own liturgy in a building whose status is determined by the church rather than by being registered with the state.[13]

The virtual invisibility of that legal framework to those getting married in an Anglican church was reflected in Anna's comment that "because that's the traditional way of doing it, you don't even ask questions … you do all

---

[7] For discussion of the relationship between state and church, see Lisa O'Connell (2019) *The Origins of the English Marriage Plot: Literature, Politics and Religion in the Eighteenth Century* (Cambridge University Press); Rebecca Probert (2020) 'State and law' in Paul Puschmann (ed) *A Cultural History of Marriage in the Age of Empires* (Bloomsbury).

[8] This was done by introducing the options of marrying in a registered place of worship or a register office. See further Rebecca Probert (2021) *Tying the Knot: The Formation of Marriage 1836–2020* (Cambridge University Press), ch 3.

[9] The key change affecting Anglican weddings was the option of giving notice at a register office as an alternative to the Anglican preliminaries. The accompanying legislation on civil registration also required clergy to submit details of the marriages they had conducted to the newly established General Register Office.

[10] For discussion of earlier proposals that would have put the Church in Wales on the same footing as other churches in Wales, see Nicholas Roberts (2011) 'The historical background to the Marriage (Wales) Act 2010' 13 *Ecclesiastical Law Journal* 39.

[11] For discussion of the subsequent divergence between the rules applying to the Church of England and the Church in Wales, see Probert (2021), 172–9.

[12] Thomas Glyn Watkin (1990) 'Vestiges of establishment: the ecclesiastical and canon law of the Church in Wales' 2 *Ecclesiastical Law Journal* 110.

[13] For the detail of these requirements, see Law Commission (2020), paras 2.64–2.109.

of the church bit and then you literally go and sit at a table while the choir is singing and sign a bit of paper". As she added:

> 'And that is the legal bit and it's such a small part of it, that if that's your own experience, you don't really realize that that's not part of the ... I guess I didn't realize that wasn't a part of the actual church wedding. That is a separate bit tacked on but in the same room.'[14]

The constraints of establishment

It is generally accepted that Anglican clergy have a duty to conduct the marriages of any persons who qualify to be married in their parish, regardless of the individuals' beliefs, unless specifically exempted from doing so. Admittedly, these exemptions encompass quite a significant number of couples: as well as being unable to conduct weddings for same-sex couples, clergy are also entitled to refuse to conduct the wedding of any person who has been divorced, any person who has undergone gender reassignment, and certain persons related by affinity.[15] Nonetheless, the duty to marry those within their parish regardless of beliefs is seen as a corollary (or in the case of the Church in Wales, a vestige) of being established.[16] As Richard, an Anglican clergyman, explained, "it's part of the Church of England's commitment to the people who live in the parish. So, we are here for everybody, whatever their religion or not". As a result, the beliefs of those marrying in an Anglican church may not align with those of the person leading the ceremony. Our study included a number of examples of this: Anna's spouse was Hindu and Fariha was Muslim. Other participants noted that they had in the past married in church despite not being particularly religious: Dawn's first marriage had taken place in a church, although she had been a Pagan since she was a teenager; Grainne, who was now a Druid, noted, "I didn't go to church, but I married in a church"; and Amanda explained that the church had been a "nice building to have a wedding in".

Yet, getting married in an Anglican church does entail expressing certain beliefs. Weddings in the Church of England are regulated by canon law as well as by statute. The canon law requires the wedding to take place according

---

[14] The assumption that signing the paperwork is 'the legal bit' is a common one, although the law in fact holds the parties to be married at the point when they exchange consent to be married.

[15] See, respectively, the Matrimonial Causes Act 1965, s 8(2), the Marriage Act 1949 ss 5B and 5A, and the Marriage (Same Sex Couples) Act 2013, ss 1(2) and 1(4).

[16] Frank Cranmer (2015) 'Wales and the law of marriage: "vestiges of establishment" revisited' 174 *Law & Justice* 96.

to one of the Church's authorized rites.[17] There is a choice of three such rites: the *Book of Common Prayer*, the *Series 1* rite, and *Common Worship*.[18]

The three rites contain the same key elements, although the language and order of *Common Worship* departs more radically from its predecessors. The cleric conducting the ceremony welcomes those present, explaining the nature of marriage within Christianity and its significance in reflecting the union between Christ and the church before asking the congregation and the couple in turn to declare if they know of any impediment to the marriage. The groom and bride vow to take each other as wife and husband, respectively, 'to have and to hold from this day forward, for better, for worse, for richer, for poorer, in sickness and in health, to love and to cherish, till death us do part, according to God's holy [ordinance/law]'.[19] The groom then places a ring on the fourth finger of the bride's left hand and makes a further declaration; in *Common Worship* the bride is given the options of making a parallel declaration on receiving the ring or giving a ring in her own right. The cleric then proclaims the parties to be husband and wife and gives a final blessing, and the newly wedded pair, along with two witnesses and the cleric, sign the marriage document. Within the ceremony, there will also be a sermon and prayers, and usually hymns and readings, although the order of these will depend on which rite is being used.

Whether that form of ceremony accords with what a couple regards as a wedding will depend on their own beliefs and traditions. For present purposes, the key point is the tension between the idea of an Anglican wedding being available 'for everybody' and a liturgy that assumes a shared faith. Put simply, those getting married in an Anglican church have to refer to God at least once in the course of the ceremony. The most modern of the three rites, *Common Worship*, is the most demanding, as each party also has to declare that they make their vows 'in the presence of God'. For those who share a belief in God, this goes to the essence of the ceremony. For those who do not, it is liable to create an uncomfortable sense of hypocrisy.[20] It is

---

[17] Canons of the Church of England, B1 and B2. For discussion of the liturgy and its implications, see Sarah Farrimond (2015) 'Church of England weddings and ritual symbolism' in Joanna Miles, Perveez Mody, and Rebecca Probert (eds) *Marriage Rites and Rights* (Hart).

[18] Faculty Office of the Archbishop of Canterbury (2010) *Anglican Marriage in England and Wales: A Guide to the Law for Clergy* (3rd ed), para 16.2.

[19] The phrasing of this part of the service is identical in all three versions save for the final word, with the *Book of Common Prayer* and *Series 1* using the word 'ordinance' and *Common Worship* using the word 'law'.

[20] This was a theme that emerged among those who had chosen a Humanist ceremony. See further Chapter 7. It was also a key theme in research commissioned by the Church of England as to why couples did not get married in church: see Gillian Oliver (2012) *The Church Weddings Handbook* (Church House Publishing, 2012).

also, as Michael Hampson has argued, potentially damaging to the Church, since 'affirming that they are full members of the church even though they know almost nothing of its life and its faith ... mocks the Christian language used in the ceremonies, devaluing its authentic use'.[21]

That tension could be resolved by allowing clergy a general discretion to determine whose weddings they conduct or by creating a form of ceremony that acknowledges that the church is providing a service to the community by hosting weddings for couples who do not share its beliefs (or indeed by both of these options together). Our point here is not that the Church of England or Church in Wales should adopt either of these approaches, but simply that neither of these options lies within the power of individual clergy. For them, establishment is a burden as well as a privilege, and it constrains how they can serve the communities in which they operate.

Quaker and Jewish weddings

Quaker weddings are far simpler than Anglican ones, although at their heart there is the same tradition of an exchange of vows. Quakers reject the idea that any priest or magistrate is needed to marry a couple. A Quaker wedding begins with a period of stillness, followed by a welcome from a member of the Society of Friends. After a further period of stillness, each of the parties takes the other by the hand and declares: 'Friends, I take this my friend [name] to be my spouse, promising, through divine assistance, to be unto [him/her] a loving and faithful spouse, so long as we both on earth shall live.' Rings may, but need not be, exchanged. The couple, along with all those present, then sign the marriage certificate.[22]

Jewish weddings are conducted in accordance with Jewish law.[23] The ceremony takes place under a canopy, or *chuppah*. A rabbi presides over the ceremony, pronouncing various benedictions over the couple. The bride and groom each sip from a cup of wine. However, the core element of the ceremony is the placing of the ring on the bride's finger by the groom while he pronounces the words 'Thou art wedded unto me according to the law of Moses and Israel'. This exchange must take place before witnesses, who must be Jewish and not closely related either to each other or to the parties to the marriage. The groom then stamps on a glass to break it.

[21] Michael Hampson (2006) *Last Rites: The End of the Church of England* (Granta Books), 16.
[22] Quakers, *A Quaker Wedding*: www.quaker.org.uk/documents/a-quaker-wedding-dl-05-2022
[23] For discussion, see Norman Doe (2018) *Comparative Religious Law* (Cambridge University Press), 280–4.

These elements of Quaker and Jewish ceremonies have been consistent over the centuries. How these ceremonies have been accommodated within the law of England and Wales has, however, changed over time, as the following sections will discuss.

From exemption to exception

An examination of the history of Quaker and Jewish weddings explains why they were treated differently. For present purposes, that history begins in the mid-17th century with the foundation of the Society of Friends and the formal readmission of Jews into the jurisdiction.[24] With the exception of Catholics, these were the only groups at that time who systematically married outside the legal framework, and Jewish communities were the only non-Christian group of numerical significance in England and Wales in the 18th century.

The evidence suggests that Jewish weddings were recognized but Quaker weddings were not.[25] Nonetheless, when the law governing weddings was put on a statutory footing in 1753, both groups were exempted from its provisions.[26] The terms of the exemption left the legal status of such weddings somewhat ambiguous, but in the 1790s it was confirmed that the ecclesiastical courts had jurisdiction to determine the validity of a Jewish marriage and that it would do so by applying Jewish law.[27] The status of a Quaker wedding remained uncertain for longer, but it was finally determined in 1829 that it would be assessed by reference to the forms of the Society of Friends.[28]

With the Marriage Act 1836, Quaker and Jewish weddings were brought within the legal framework rather than being exempted from it.[29] From 1837 they had to be preceded by civil preliminaries and a specific person was tasked with their registration. But the Act also echoed the ambiguities of its predecessor in providing that Quakers and Jews could 'continue to contract and solemnize marriages' according to their own 'usages'.[30]

---

[24] See, respectively, William C. Braithwaite (1912) *The Beginnings of Quakerism* (Macmillan & Co Ltd) and H.S.Q. Henriques, 'Jewish marriages and the English law' (1908) 20 *The Jewish Quarterly Review* 391.

[25] Probert (2009), ch 4.

[26] Clandestine Marriages Act 1753, s 18.

[27] *Lindo v Belisario* (1796) 1 Hag Con (App) 7; 161 ER 636. The case law also demonstrated that the requirements of Jewish law could be exacting: the possibility of recognition did not mean that a marriage would necessarily be upheld as valid: see *Goldsmid v Bromer* (1798) 1 Hag Con 324; 161 ER 568.

[28] *Deane v Thomas* (1829) M & M 361; 173 ER 1189. For discussion of the limitations of this as an authority, see Probert (2009), 330.

[29] Probert (2021), 44–5.

[30] Marriage Act 1836, s 2.

As a result, Quaker and Jewish weddings did not need to take place in a specific building, include the words prescribed by statute, or have a civil registrar present.[31]

The two rabbis who participated in our study, Adam and Rachael, were conscious that they enjoyed far greater freedom than other religious groups as to where they could conduct marriages. Adam recalled being reassured by the local registration officers as to the legality of a Jewish wedding at a beach hut, adding, "I'm not even sure ... that most of our weddings nowadays take place in the synagogue". Rachael had conducted a wedding in a field. She took the view that the freedoms they enjoyed should be extended to other groups.

However, in certain respects Quaker and Jewish weddings are *less* free from regulation than others. In the sections that follow, we outline the constraints of adherence, authority, and usages before considering the status of Quaker and Jewish weddings conducted outside the legal framework.

The constraints of adherence

Under the 1836 Act, the special provisions applicable to Quaker and Jewish weddings were only applicable where *both* parties were Quaker or Jewish.[32] This was a significant restriction given that no other religious weddings were limited in this way, although it was consistent with the views of the Society of Friends and the Jewish community on 'marrying out'.[33]

By the mid-19th century, however, declining numbers led to a change of policy by the Society of Friends.[34] Legislation was passed in 1860 and 1872 to amend the 1836 Act, first to allow those who 'professed with' or were 'of the persuasion of' the Society of Friends to marry according to its usages and then to allow the Society to decide for itself who it would permit to do so.[35] No such change was made to Jewish weddings, and 'outmarriage' was identified by 20th-century demographers as one of the factors contributing to a decline in the number of weddings taking place in synagogues.[36]

---

[31] For discussion of how these freedoms were exercised in practice, see Probert (2021), 76–80.

[32] Marriage Act 1836, s 2.

[33] See, for example, Elizabeth Isichei (1970) *Victorian Quakers* (Oxford University Press), 115; Michael Clark (2005) *Identity and Equality: The Anglo-Jewish Community in the Post-Emancipation Era, 1858–1887* (DPhil thesis, Oxford).

[34] See John Stephenson Rowntree (1859) *Quakerism Past and Present: An Inquiry into the Causes of Its Decline in Great Britain and Ireland* (Smith, Elder & Co).

[35] See, respectively, the Marriage (Society of Friends) Act 1860 and the Marriage (Society of Friends) Act 1872. For discussion of these changes, see Probert (2021), 104–5.

[36] S.J. Prais and Marlena Schmool (1967) 'Statistics of Jewish marriage in Great Britain: 1901–1965' 9 *Jewish Journal of Sociology* 151, and (1970) 'Synagogue marriages in Great

It still remains the case that Jewish marriages may only be celebrated between 'two persons professing the Jewish religion',[37] although the gender neutrality of this provision signals the subsequent acceptance of same-sex marriage within certain strands of Judaism. Within our sample, David had been unable to have his legal wedding according to Jewish usages because he was marrying a Catholic. Reflecting on the Law Commission's proposal that there should be no *legal* restriction on the availability of Jewish weddings,[38] he noted that it remained to be seen whether that would lead to any change in religious practice. For him, however, that was the most important of the changes being proposed.

The constraints of authority

The 1836 Act did not simply state that Quaker and Jewish weddings were to be recognized. Instead, it put a framework in place whereby they could be recognized. A key element of this new framework was the civil registration of all marriages. The fact that the system was dependent on the provision of physical register books meant that those with the power and responsibility to register marriages had to be identified in advance. And this in turn required rules to be put in place as to who would identify such persons.

For Quaker marriages, it was the role of the recording clerk of the Society of Friends, while for Jewish marriages, it was the President of the London Committee of Deputies of the British Jews.[39] The underlying assumption was that these individuals had sufficient oversight of their co-religionists, and sufficient authority, to be entrusted with this role. At the same time, it gave them a powerful tool to determine – and therefore to control – who exactly counted as either Quaker or Jewish.

This can be illustrated by showing what happened when a group broke away from the mainstream. Within Quakerism, this occurred as early as 1839 when a group of 'Evangelical Friends' split from the Society.[40] With

---

Britain: 1966–8' 12 *Jewish Journal of Sociology* 21; Barry Kosmin and Stanley Waterman (1986) 'Recent trends in Anglo-Jewish marriages' 28 *Jewish Journal of Sociology* 51.

[37] Marriage Act 1949, s 26.

[38] Law Commission (2020), para 6.70; see also Law Commission (2022) *Celebrating Marriage: A New Weddings Law* (19 July), para 5.119, recommending that there should be no legal limitations on who can marry in an Anglican, Jewish, or Quaker wedding but that 'like all religious groups', Jewish and Quaker groups 'will continue to be able to impose their own requirements about whose ceremonies they will conduct, as a matter of their own practice'.

[39] Births and Deaths Registration Act 1836, s 30.

[40] John Punshon (1984) *Portrait in Grey: A Short History of the Quakers* (Quaker Home Service), 198.

no mechanism to nominate its own registering officers, it had to pursue the alternative of registering its place of worship. The following year, Judaism faced a similar split when a breakaway group announced their intention to set up a new synagogue in West London, 'where a revised service may be performed … in a manner more calculated to inspire feelings of devotion'.[41] In the view of the Chief Rabbi, this new group was not professing the Jewish religion,[42] and the President accordingly refused to certify the secretary to the Registrar General.[43] This left members of the West London Synagogue without *any* means of marrying in accordance with their beliefs, since there was no option of registering the synagogue for weddings at this time.[44] But when Parliament reconsidered the terms of the 1836 Act in the 1850s, it conferred on the West London Synagogue the power to certify not only its own secretaries but also those belonging to other synagogues.[45] The same approach was adopted when a new strand of Liberal Judaism emerged,[46] although in this case almost half a century elapsed before their main synagogue (in St John's Wood) was given the power to certify its own secretary and that of any synagogue connected with it.[47]

Both Adam and Rachael noted that the process of certification within their respective organizations was relatively straightforward. However, while Adam had been certified as a marriage secretary when he was the rabbi for a North London synagogue, Rachael had not taken on that role, noting: "I've always felt that I have enough to do with the Jewish stuff and I've always, you know, whichever synagogue I've been in, we've had our lay members who have been secretaries for the marriage. They look after the civil stuff." As that indicates, if they are not also appointed as a secretary, a rabbi does not necessarily have any legal responsibility – or indeed any power – to ensure that a marriage is subsequently registered. And as David described,

---

[41] Quoted by David Katz (1994) *The Jews in the History of England 1485–1850* (Oxford University Press), 335.

[42] The constitution of the Board of Deputies required the President to ascertain the view of the relevant ecclesiastical authorities as to whether a synagogue could be described as 'Jewish'. The relevant ecclesiastical authorities were either the haham or other designated official of the Sephardim, or the Chief Rabbi: Geoffrey Alderman (1992) *Modern British Jewry* (Clarendon Press), 40.

[43] David Feldman (1994) *Englishmen and Jews: Social Relations and Political Culture, 1840–1914* (Yale University Press), 24.

[44] This changed with the Places of Worship Registration Act 1855: see Probert (2021), 101–2.

[45] Marriage and Registration Act 1856, s 22. See now Marriage Act 1949, s 67(b).

[46] For discussion of the emergence of Liberal Judaism, see Alderman (1992), 206–8.

[47] Marriage (Secretaries of Synagogues) Act 1959.

there are also rabbis who offer wedding ceremonies "where people have fallen outside what is offered by mainstream Judaism", who are unlikely to have the authority to conduct legal weddings.[48]

The constraints of usages

As noted earlier, the 1836 Act referred to Quaker and Jewish weddings being celebrated according to their own 'usages'.[49] This reference to usages, which is repeated in the 1949 Act, has generally been interpreted as the law recognizing Quaker and Jewish weddings. But it could also be seen as requiring them to take place in a particular form – something that is not required of other non-Anglican groups.

Indeed, when giving evidence to the 1868 Royal Commission, one Jewish Member of Parliament complained that the treatment of Jewish marriages went against the policy of the 1836 Act. While others, he said, could

> marry according to their own religious views, without any heed or interference by the State in what may be properly considered as the spiritual element ... [t]his principle is abandoned in the case of the Jews, for they, in compliance with these Acts, are required to marry according to their 'usages'.[50]

Requiring Quaker and Jewish marriages to be conducted according to their usages could be seen as the functional equivalent of requiring weddings in registered religious building to include certain prescribed words and for witnesses to be in attendance, given that both groups have their own prescribed words and requirements for witnesses.

However, both Adam and Rachael saw Jewish usages as going beyond these basic requirements. As Adam noted, the format of a Jewish wedding ceremony is always exactly the same:

> 'It's not à la carte. You know, couples do sort of come along and they say "We'd like to do this, we'd like to do that". Most of our rabbis would have to keep a fairly firm line and say "Look, you know, this is how it's going to be and take it or leave it".'

---

[48] David commented on one such rabbi: "I think he was ordained – I mean, we use that word in Judaism but it doesn't quite do the trick – by the Progressive movement, but then hasn't run a congregation."

[49] Marriage Act 1836, s 2.

[50] *Report of the Royal Commission on the Laws of Marriage 1868* [4059], App 1, 11.

Rachael reported that the rules as to who could be a witness had proved particularly problematic when the numbers who could attend a wedding were limited; when those present did not qualify, she had resorted to suggesting that the couple simply bring in anybody who was "hanging around outside".

This raises the question as to the status of a Quaker or Jewish wedding that does *not* comply with their respective usages. While a number of scholars have claimed that such a marriage would be void,[51] that is on the basis of the pre-1836 case law. At that time, conformity with Quaker and Jewish practices had to be the touchstone of validity, because there was no other basis by which the validity of such marriages could have been assessed. But both the 1836 Act and the 1949 Act set out the grounds on which a marriage can be declared void, and the courts have taken the view that a marriage cannot be declared void on grounds that are not set out in the statute. While both Acts assumed that Quaker and Jewish marriages would be conducted in accordance with their usages, neither stated that non-compliance with such usages would render a marriage void. Moreover, it is difficult to see what interest the state would have in enforcing religious conformity in this way.

In practice, the scope for marriages to be challenged on the basis of non-compliance with the required usages has been limited by the requirement that the person responsible for registering the marriage satisfy themselves that the proceedings did conform to the relevant usages. Once the marriage is registered, this is taken as evidence that the relevant usages had been observed. Moreover, while the law does not require the person responsible for registering a Quaker or Jewish wedding to be present at it, in practice they do usually attend and are therefore able to ensure that all necessary usages are observed. While Rachael reported conducting a ceremony without a marriage secretary being present, it was clear that this was an exception: "It was very odd, and I didn't feel comfortable doing it at all, because, you know, I do feel a great responsibility to make sure that I have obeyed the law. I don't want to produce a couple that aren't married."

Non-recognition of ceremonies conducted outside the legal framework

In this section, we turn to the status of ceremonies that are conducted according to Jewish usages but outside the legal framework.[52] The evidence here suggests that it is a fallacy to assume that Jewish weddings are automatically accorded legal recognition.

---

[51] Henriques (1908); Joseph Jackson (1969) *The Formation and Annulment of Marriage* (Butterworths, 2nd ed), 201.

[52] While the same considerations could in principle apply to Quaker ceremonies, in practice we are not aware of such ceremonies being conducted outside the legal framework.

The late 19th century saw a significant number of Jewish weddings being conducted outside the framework of the 1836 Act in the wake of increasing numbers of migrants from Poland and Russia arriving in England.[53] When these cases came before the courts, deserted wives seeking maintenance from errant husbands received short shrift in the magistrates' courts. Pleas that the ceremony had been conducted in accordance with Jewish law fell on deaf ears: the view was taken that maintenance could only be ordered if there was a lawful marriage, and a lawful marriage required notice to have been given to the registrar.[54]

However, it does not follow that a Jewish marriage will be *void* if the parties have not given notice. Under both the 1836 Act and the 1949 Act, only a 'knowing and wilful' failure to give notice results in a marriage being void.[55] In *Nathan v Woolf*, a Jewish marriage was upheld on the basis that there was no evidence that the wife had 'knowingly and wilfully' failed to comply with the requirement to give notice.[56] From a modern perspective, however, the more difficult question may be what is sufficient to bring a Jewish ceremony within the framework of the law for the purpose of it being held to be a void marriage rather than a non-qualifying ceremony.[57] In the absence of notice being given, it is difficult to see any way in which a Jewish ceremony could be deemed to be conducted 'under the provisions' of the 1949 Act other than by being conducted according to Jewish usages. The choice therefore lies between treating Jewish ceremonies more harshly than others (by making a failure to give notice result in a non-qualifying ceremony) or much more generously (by holding a ceremony conducted according to religious usages to be valid).

The issue is not a hypothetical one. While Adam confirmed that the usual practice was not to allow a wedding to go ahead unless the civil preliminaries had been completed and "the civil registration" was taking place at the same time, he noted that he had "occasionally been a bit more flexible" where

---

[53] For discussion, see David Englander (1992) '*Stille huppah* (quiet marriage) among Jewish immigrants in Britain' 34 *Jewish Journal of Sociology* 85; Rainer Liedtke (1998) *Jewish Welfare in Hamburg and Manchester, c. 1850–1914* (Oxford University Press), 155–6.

[54] See, for example, *Leeds Times* (1894) 'A Jewish marriage turns to be no legal marriage at all', 1 December; *Derby Daily Telegraph* (1904) 'Under the canopy: Jewish marriage practices' 3 August.

[55] Marriage Act 1836, s 42; Marriage Act 1949, s 49.

[56] (1899) 15 TLR 250. The judge in that case also confirmed that Jewish marriages were subject to the same annulling provision as all other marriages.

[57] As per the decision of the Court of Appeal in *AG v Akhter and Khan* [2020] EWCA Civ 122.

the marriage involved a partner from another country.[58] In addition, when referring to the COVID-19 pandemic, he explained that

> 'because of this, you know, amazing chaos that's been going on this year, I've had to say to people "Look, whilst we would normally insist that the civil registration takes place concurrently with the religious ceremony, in these circumstances, provided we have an assurance that as soon as possible thereafter, if it can be done, that you'll get married in a registry office ceremony". Then we've allowed a separation of the two ceremonies ... we're just trying not to make life more unpleasant and frustrating for people than is absolutely necessary to do.'

Such exceptional circumstances apart, the evidence suggests that Quaker and Jewish marriages today are almost invariably conducted in conformity with the legal framework. Such conformity provides further evidence that the threat of criminal sanctions is not necessary to secure compliance.[59]

Conclusion

While Anglican, Jewish, and Quaker weddings all have certain privileges that are not accorded to other religious groups, they are also subject to particular constraints that do not apply to other religious groups. The established status of the Church of England, and the vestiges of establishment within the Church in Wales, mean that it alone cannot refuse to conduct weddings for those who do not share its beliefs. At the same time, couples marrying according to Anglican rites have to invoke a god in whom they may or may not believe. For Quakers and Jews, the law should be seen as having adopted a different model of regulation, rather than no regulation at all – one based on regulation by an overarching organization rather than on regulation of the place of marriage. The privileges that the Marriage Acts of 1836 and 1949 conferred were no doubt appreciated by the bodies named in the legislation. But for individual Quakers and Jews, the regulations may have seemed more obvious than the freedoms.

It is also important to note that the special treatment of Jewish and Quaker weddings is simply the result of historical happenstance rather than the nature of the ceremony. While Adam thought that the recognition of Jewish

---

[58] This was largely on account of the residence requirement: on which, see Rebecca Probert, Rajnaara C. Akhtar, and Sharon Blake (2021) *When Is a Wedding Not a Marriage? A Briefing Paper for the Law Commission*, 2.20.

[59] No offence is committed where a Quaker or Jewish ceremony takes place outside the framework of the Marriage Act 1949.

weddings was "because the religious ceremony phenomenologically mirrors what goes on in a registry office", the differences between Anglican, Quaker, and Jewish weddings, or indeed between Quaker and Jewish weddings and a civil wedding in a register office, are as striking as the similarities. An Anglican wedding involves the parties being asked to declare if there is any impediment to the marriage and a civil wedding requires the parties to make a declaration that they are free to marry, but no such declaration is required in a Quaker or Jewish ceremony. In Anglican and Quaker weddings, the bride and groom exchange vows; in Orthodox Judaism, only the groom is required to speak. The giving and receiving of a ring is central to a Jewish wedding, usual in an Anglican one, and optional in a Quaker one. In other words, there is no common core underpinning the wedding ceremonies of these three religious groups. Yet the law has for centuries been content to accept an Anglican, Quaker, or Jewish couple as being married at the point at which they are regarded as married by their respective religions. That, more than anything else, is why they are justifiably seen as privileged.

3

Christian Weddings in Registered Places of Worship

'Our weddings are normally at church and are legally binding.'[1]

Introduction

As a matter of law, Christian weddings – excepting Anglican and Quaker weddings, discussed in Chapter 2 – stand on exactly the same footing as those of other faiths. In essence, any religious group is able to register its place of worship for weddings, subject to certain conditions being fulfilled.[2] Once that is done, weddings may be celebrated there in whatever ceremony the couple may choose, as long as each party makes a declaration that they are free to marry, and consents to marry, according to one of the forms set out in the Act.[3] These 'prescribed words' must be spoken in the presence of two witnesses and either a civil registrar or an authorized person appointed by the governing body of the registered place of worship.[4]

Yet our Christian participants tended to have a very different view of weddings in registered places of worship from that expressed by Buddhists, Hindus, Muslims, and Sikhs. The opening quote in this chapter illustrates how Christian participants saw the law as enabling them to marry in accordance with their beliefs. The reason for this is simple: as we describe in the next section, since the legal requirements were designed for Christian weddings, it is easier for Christian weddings to comply with those requirements and

---

[1] Simon, Baptist minister.
[2] In order to be registered, a place of worship must (1) be certified as a place of worship under the Places of Worship Registration Act 1855; (2) consist of a building (or part of a building); and (3) have the support of 20 householders who use the building as their usual place of public religious worship: Marriage Act 1949, s 41.
[3] Marriage Act 1949, s 44.
[4] Marriage Act 1949, ss 43 and 43B.

for those requirements to be seen as being rooted in religious observance rather than legal prescriptions.[5]

There are, it should be noted, varying views within Christianity as to how a marriage should be formed.[6] To take only the most basic of distinctions, the Catholic Church regards marriage as a sacrament, has a set liturgy for the ceremony, and requires the ceremony to be conducted in the presence of a priest in order to be religiously valid; Protestant churches, by contrast, do not regard marriage as a sacrament, may or may not have a formal liturgy,[7] and hold differing views on whether the presence of a minister is required.

However, as we shall show, the law was designed for the diverse forms that a Christian wedding might take. In this chapter, we focus on why the option of getting married in a registered place of worship works better for Christian groups than it does for those of other faiths. We begin by looking at why this option was introduced and why it was framed in such a way as to allow couples to marry 'according to such form and ceremony' as they saw 'fit to adopt'[8] rather than in accordance with specific religious rites, but how it was nonetheless designed with Christian weddings in mind. We then go on to show how different types of Christian weddings operated within that legal framework and how the option of getting married in a registered place of worship worked better for some Christian groups than for others. In the final section, we turn to the data from the Nuffield Foundation-funded project to show how getting married in a Christian registered place of worship is understood today.

A scheme designed for Christian weddings

As explained in Chapter 2, before the Marriage Act 1836, the law only formally made provision for Anglican weddings. This lack of provision was unsurprising. The Quakers apart, Protestant Dissenters had not developed

---

[5]   That experience is likely to be replicated across much of Europe: the rules governing entry into marriage were originally governed by the canon law of either the Catholic or Orthodox church: see Maria V. Antokolskaia (2003) 'Development of family law in Western and Eastern Europe: common origins, common driving forces, common tendencies' 28 *Journal of Family History* 52.

[6]   On which see Norman Doe (2013) *Christian Law* (Cambridge University Press), 254–60. There are also differences in terms of willingness to conduct same-sex weddings or weddings involving a partner who has been divorced.

[7]   The Unitarian Church, for example, explains: 'we don't have a standard marriage ceremony. Instead, our talented ministers work with you to determine exactly what your wedding sounds, looks and feels like. We can provide a more traditional service if you like, but we're equally happy providing a more innovative service': The Unitarians, 'Weddings': www.unitarian.org.uk/your-special-event/weddings/

[8]   Marriage Act 1836, s 20.

their own distinct marriage rites and had almost invariably married in the parish church even before the Clandestine Marriages Act 1753, while the legal status of the small Catholic population was precarious, with their right to worship not recognized by law.[9]

The virtual monopoly of the Church of England began to be challenged in the early decades of the 19th century, and the Marriage Act 1836 provided both Protestant Dissenters and Catholics with an alternative to being married in the Church of England by allowing certified places of worship to be registered for weddings. There was, however, an important difference between providing an alternative and formally recognizing the wedding ceremonies of Protestant Dissenters and Catholics per se. The Act conferred no authority on Dissenting ministers or Catholic priests to conduct weddings: every wedding in a registered place of worship had to be attended by a civil registrar. Nor did it require such weddings to be conducted according to religious rites. Instead, weddings were to be celebrated 'according to such form and ceremony' as the couple 'may see fit to adopt', subject to the inclusion of prescribed declarations and vows.[10]

This approach reflected the way in which the campaign for reform had been framed.[11] The diversity of Dissent meant that those calling for reform had very different ideas about how they wanted to marry and the alternative model of regulating a specific group or groups would never have worked for them.[12] Not only was there a plethora of different groups, but many individual churches were fiercely independent, existing outside any denominational organization. All that united them was a desire for an alternative to getting married in the Church of England.[13]

From the start, then, the 1836 framework was designed to ensure that no one was required to marry in a way that was incompatible with their conscience. Its neutral framing was more radical than simply adding to the list of groups whose marriages would be recognized, as had occurred in other parts of the United Kingdom when similar challenges arose.[14] It was,

---

[9]   Freedom of worship was only secured by the Roman Catholic Relief Act 1791. On Catholic marriages before and after the 1753 Act, see Rebecca Probert (2009) *Marriage Law and Practice in the Long Eighteenth Century: A Reassessment* (Cambridge University Press), chs 4 and 9.

[10] Marriage Act 1836, s 20.

[11] On which see Rebecca Probert (2021) *Tying the Knot: The Formation of Marriage, 1836–2020* (Cambridge University Press), ch 2.

[12] That alternative model was, however, adopted for Quakers: see Chapter 2.

[13] For discussion of the range of views within Dissent, see further Rebecca Probert (2022) 'Secular or sacred? The ambiguity of "civil" marriage in the Marriage Act 1836' 43 *Journal of Legal History* 136.

[14] Rebecca Probert, Maebh Harding, and Brian Dempsey (2018) 'A uniform law of marriage? The 1868 Royal Commission reconsidered' 30 *Child and Family Law Quarterly* 217.

nonetheless, devised primarily with Christian weddings in mind. First, the possibility of registering a place of worship for weddings depended on it being certified as a place of worship in the first place. Since only Christian places of worship could be certified as such,[15] only Christian places of worship could be registered for weddings. Second, the prescribed words, while shorn of any explicitly religious references, were closely modelled on the structure and form of the marriage service of the Church of England as set out in the *Book of Common Prayer*.[16]

The fact that the words were the same as those prescribed for weddings in register offices has led some to categorize weddings in registered places of worship as 'civil' ones.[17] It is therefore of some significance that the legislation did not stipulate that those getting married in a registered place of worship should marry in the same form as in a register office; rather, the prescribed words are set out in the section dealing with weddings in registered places of worship, and the section introducing the possibility of marrying in the register office merely notes that the parties are to marry 'making the Declaration and using the Form of Words herein-before provided in the Case of Marriage in any such registered Building'.[18] In other words, the civil wedding in a register office could also be described as a Christian-based ceremony. This point had not escaped the notice of David: "It always struck me as slightly ironic that even the sort of standard civil ceremony is very much aping the *Book of Common Prayer*, you know, in its wording. You know, one feels it and it's sort of there and present in the room."

How the scheme worked for different Christian weddings

The fact that the 1836 Act was devised with Christian weddings in mind did not mean it worked equally for different Christian groups. Three key factors determined whether groups were able to avail themselves of the option of registering their place of worship for weddings and how that option was experienced.

The first was whether any given group had a sufficient critical mass in a given area to be able to afford its own building and sufficient support

---

[15] Toleration Act 1688; Roman Catholic Relief Act 1791; Places of Religious Worship Act 1812. For discussion of the significance attached to location, see Wendy Kennett (2015) 'The place of worship in solemnization of a marriage' 30 *Journal of Law and Religion* 260.

[16] For analysis of the similarities and differences between the *Book of Common Prayer* and the prescribed words, see Probert (2022).

[17] See, for example, Thomas Glyn Watkin (1990) 'Vestiges of establishment: the ecclesiastical and canon law of the Church in Wales' 2 *Ecclesiastical Law Journal* 110, 111.

[18] Marriage Act 1836, s 21.

for that building to be registered for weddings.[19] Making provision for a wedding to be conducted in a registered place of worship was an indirect means of controlling which groups could conduct weddings. Legislators would have been fully aware that many religious groups did not have a place of worship capable of satisfying the conditions for registration.[20] The buildings-based model in essence favoured those groups that operated in a similar way to the Church of England in terms of having a dedicated place of worship (although an early amendment to the 1836 Act allowed Catholic places of worship to be registered even if they did not constitute a separate building).[21] Throughout the 19th century, many places of worship remained unregistered,[22] and many couples who wanted to marry in their place of worship therefore had to decide whether to have a separate legally recognized wedding in a register office or an Anglican church.[23]

The second factor was whether any given denomination had specific requirements for a religiously recognized ceremony with which the prescribed words might conflict. To the extent that Protestant Dissenters were starting with a blank slate in 1837, their new wedding services could be constructed around the prescribed words rather than these having to be inserted into an existing liturgy. Where groups had already devised their own wedding services, these tended to be just as closely based on the *Book of Common Prayer* as the prescribed words were. Either way, incorporating the prescribed words was a simple enough matter.[24]

For Catholics, the position was rather different. They were not starting with a blank slate, since they had their own long-established liturgies that predated the *Book of Common Prayer*. Of course, these liturgies had shaped the structure and form of the marriage service of the Church of England,[25] which had in turn shaped the prescribed words, so they would still have had a certain familiarity for Catholics. However, if both the Catholic liturgy

---

[19]   See further Probert (2021), ch 3.

[20]   See *A Return of the Number of Registered Dissenting Meeting-houses and Roman Catholic Chapels in England and Wales* (1836) 14 July, House of Commons Papers, Vol 40, 267–310 which demonstrated that many Dissenters met for worship in rooms within buildings that would not qualify to be registered.

[21]   Births and Deaths Registration Act 1837, s 35. See Probert (2021), 60.

[22]   For discussion of local variations in registration, see Michael Watts (1995) *The Dissenters* (Oxford University Press), 664.

[23]   See further Rebecca Probert (2021) 'Interpreting choices: what can we infer from where our ancestors married?' 5 *Journal of Genealogy and Family History* 75.

[24]   For examples of post-1836 marriage liturgies, see Probert (2022).

[25]   On the evolution of liturgy, see Kenneth W. Stevenson (1987) *To Join Together: The Rite of Marriage* (Pueblo Publishing Company); Mark Searle and Kenneth W. Stevenson (1992) *Documents of the Marriage Liturgy* (The Liturgical Press).

and the prescribed words had to be said exactly, even a minor difference in phrasing meant that they had to be said separately.

Catholics therefore perceived a clear difference between that part of the ceremony that was conducted according to their own religious rites and 'the civil portion of the ceremony' performed before the registrar.[26] The separation was not merely conceptual but also physical: as one 19th-century legal commentator explained, the practice of the parties was to 'leave the body of the church' after the Catholic rite had been performed and repeat the prescribed words to the registrar in the sacristy or vestry.[27] But the result was that Catholics had first to declare that they were free to marry and that they took each other as husband and wife before a priest, and then do the same before the registrar.

The fact that the two parts of the ceremony were so similar was seen as undermining both. For some, such repetition made the civil part of the ceremony 'ludicrous';[28] for others, it was 'offensive' in 'implying insufficiency in the Sacramental form'.[29] As one Catholic priest noted of the declaration to the registrar, either the parties were making a solemn declaration that they knew of no reason 'why they may not contract a marriage which they have already contracted'[30] or they were acknowledging that the Catholic rite was of no effect in the eyes of the law. Moreover, the fact the words that had to be repeated before the registrar were exactly the same as those that had to be exchanged in a register office led the priest to conclude 'that the law altogether ignores the Catholic marriage and supersedes it by one of its own'.[31]

That brings us on to the third factor that influenced how the option of getting married in a registered place of worship operated: whether a religious group accorded a specific role to a priest or minister with which the presence of a registrar might compete. Some Dissenting groups had no ordained ministry and were content to say the prescribed words before the registrar, and it was perfectly valid for the registrar to marry the couple 'without any

---

[26] 'Marriage', *The Tablet* (1887) 17 September, 460.

[27] James T. Hammick (1887) *The Marriage Law of England: A Practical Treatise on the Legal Incidents Connected with the Law of Constitution of the Matrimonial Contract* (Shaw & Sons), 147–8.

[28] See the submission of Archbishop Manning and the Roman Catholic Bishops of England: *Report of the Royal Commission on the Laws of Marriage 1868* [4059] App 1, 44.

[29] 'Marriages of Nonconformists Bill', *The Tablet* (1891) 14 March, 422. See also 'The Registrar at Catholic Marriages', *The Tablet* (1888) 21 April, 650 ('an indignity to Catholics') and 'Can We Accept Them', *The Tablet* (1891) 21 March, 455 ('superfluous insult').

[30] 'Baby Farming and the Law of Marriage', *The Tablet* (1879) 25 October, 535.

[31] *The Tablet* (1879).

religious observance whatever' if a minister was unable to attend.[32] For others, however, the role of the registrar was in conflict with that of the minister or priest. A letter in *The Tablet* noted that it was a 'grievous insult' to a Catholic priest 'that a mere layman should be called in to ratify his work'.[33] Others saw the registrar as actually conducting the wedding, 'while the minister only accorded a benediction on the union'.[34] One Member of Parliament went so far as to argue that those marrying in registered places of worship did not have the option of being married by 'any spiritual adviser', but that 'the marriage must be conducted by some lawyer's clerk, who may come in a fit state to marry, or in a state more spirituous than spiritual'.[35]

Throughout the 1880s and 1890s, there was a campaign to dispense with the presence of the registrar in registered places of worship.[36] This resulted in the passage of the Marriage Act 1898, which established the procedure for 'authorised persons' to be appointed.[37] While an authorized person did not have to be a minister or priest, being in essence a substitute for the civil registrar, this new option proved most popular among those religious groups that wanted their ministers to have the same status as Church of England clergy.[38]

With a few minor changes, this framework remains in place today. The Marriage Act 1949 largely consolidated the terms of the 1836 Act, with no real change so far as weddings in Christian registered places of worship were concerned. Various minor amendments were subsequently made to the conditions determining which places of worship could be registered[39] and who could marry in any given registered place of worship.[40] Provision was made for alternative versions of the prescribed words,[41] but not to

---

[32] *Liverpool Mercury* (1886) 1 September, 5.

[33] 'The Marriage Laws and Catholics', *The Tablet* (1879) 8 November, 589.

[34] *Sheffield Evening Telegraph* (1899), 'A Doubtful Privilege', 10 April, 3.

[35] Hansard, HC Deb, 24 February 1891, Vol 350, col 1542 (Mr Atkinson).

[36] See further Probert (2021), ch 5.

[37] See further Rebecca Probert, Rajnaara C. Akhtar, Sharon Blake, Vishal Vora, and Tania Barton (2021) 'The importance of being authorized: the genesis, limitations and legacy of the Marriage Act, 1898' 10 *Oxford Journal of Law and Religion* 394.

[38] Probert (2021), ch 6.

[39] See the Marriage Acts Amendment Act 1958, which removed the condition that a place of worship had to have been used as such for a year before it could be registered, and substituted a requirement that a civil registrar should attend weddings in its first year of operation; the Sharing of Church Buildings Act 1969; and the Marriage (Registration of Buildings) Act 1990, which removed the condition that a place of worship had to be a 'separate' building.

[40] See the Marriage Act 1949 (Amendment) Act 1954, which amended the conditions governing when a couple could marry in a registered place of worship in a different registration district.

[41] Marriage Ceremony (Prescribed Words) Act 1996 (on which see the section 'The invisibility of the prescribed words').

the necessity of their inclusion, and the role of the authorized person remained unaltered.[42]

Perceptions of Christian weddings in registered places of worship today

It was clear from the participants in the Nuffield Foundation-funded study that the three factors discussed earlier – whether the group has a building that can be registered for weddings, the role of the authorized person, and the requirements of the ceremony – still exert an influence on how the option of getting married in a registered place of worship works for different Christian groups. However, the vast majority of Christian places of worship are now registered for weddings, many have appointed an authorized person, and the prescribed words have been absorbed into their marriage services to the extent that they are no longer visible. In this section, we put the experiences of our participants into the context of these broader religious and legal structures to show the factors that shape the experience of getting married in a Christian place of worship today, and why our participants regarded the law as recognizing their religious ceremonies.

The number of registered places of worship

The necessity for a religious group to have a place of worship that can be registered for weddings remains a significant limitation for many Christian groups. Tom, for example, reported that his Evangelical Christian fellowship did not have its own building and so met in a local school. Dan also gave the example of a local Catholic congregation that met in a school and whose members accordingly "couldn't have a wedding where they have their Sunday service, because it wasn't an authorized building".

For Sam, the issue was not a lack of buildings but the limitations in terms of which buildings could be registered for weddings. He was a member of the Church of Jesus Christ of Latter-Day Saints, whose temples could not be registered for weddings because they were only open to members, precluding the possibility of fulfilling the condition of being places of *public* religious worship.[43] As a result, Sam's legal wedding had taken place in one of their

---

42 A minor difference is that they are now responsible for ensuring that the marriage schedule is returned to be registered, rather than for entering the marriage into a register book: The Registration of Marriages Regulations 2021, SI 2021 No 411.

43 *Church of Jesus Christ of Latter-Day Saints v Henning (Valuation Officer)* [1964] AC 420, upheld in *Gallagher (Valuation Officer) v Church of Jesus Christ of Latter-Day Saints* [2008] UKHL 56. For discussion of this restriction, see Anthony Bradney (1993) *Religions, Rights and Laws* (Leicester University Press), 41.

'chapels' that was registered for weddings, and he had a further ceremony in one of their temples. While he described the first as a religious ceremony, it was the second in which he saw himself as making the more significant commitment to his wife "for all eternity".

That said, the majority of Christian places of worship *are* registered for weddings. With over 22,000 places of worship registered by Christian denominations across England and Wales, there is no registration district without a place of worship registered by at least one Christian denomination.[44]

That in turn affects the options available to those groups that do not have their own building. The legal framework facilitates interdenominational cooperation: a place of worship may be registered *by* a particular group, but it is not registered *for* weddings conducted according to the rites of that group. It is open to the minister or trustees of each individual building to decide who may marry there and what form the wedding can take.[45] If the group wishes to host weddings for another denomination, it may do so. Tom's Evangelical Christian fellowship had benefited from such cooperation: as he explained, "we have relationships with other fellowships who very kindly have churches that will allow us to conduct services there".

While there is nothing in the legal framework to limit such cooperation to Christian groups, in reality this is only viable where there is sufficient common ground between the host building and the couple seeking to marry there. While the high number of places of worship registered by Christian groups does not guarantee cooperation, it increases the likelihood of a couple being able to find a place of worship in which they can marry.

The supportive role of the authorized person

Only one of our non-Anglican Christian interviewees, Dan, mentioned a civil registrar being present at his wedding. The other three had all married in the presence of an authorized person. Those conducting weddings were similarly either authorized persons or had experience of working alongside an authorized person. As Simon explained, "I am the minister and I am doing the legal part of it as well".

The presence of an authorized person, rather than a civil registrar, was significant for a number of reasons. First, there was no state employee present to remind the couple that it was compliance with the legal requirements that created a marriage. Second, authorized persons tended to be appointed

---

[44] UK Government (2015) 'Places of worship registered for marriage' (15 March): www. gov.uk/government/publications/places-of-worship-registered-for-marriage

[45] Marriage Act 1949, s 44(1).

from the congregation, ensuring that the couple getting married knew that those involved in the ceremony shared their beliefs.[46] Sarah, for example, described how her wedding in a Baptist church had taken place in the presence of both a minister and "the lovely lady at the church, who is the approved person", and John similarly explained that the persons chosen to be authorized would be "regular attenders" at mass. Third, there was a sense that the authorized person was there to support the priest or minister rather than playing an active role in leading the service. Mary noted the presence of "the person that helps the priest to make sure that all the registrations and everything were undertaken correctly". In addition to his role as a minister, Simon had also taken on a supportive role for other ministers, describing how he had been "involved in weddings where another minister has come and led it and I've just been there to be the authorized person and to deal with the paperwork side". Tom had experienced this from the other side as the minister coming in to perform a wedding but without the authorization to register it; he noted that the authorized person "will be there listening and will actually do all the legal side of it". All of these factors would have contributed to minimizing the intrusion of the legal requirements into the ceremony and supporting these participants' sense that the law recognized their religious ceremonies.

The option of appointing an authorized person is not limited to Christian places of worship. Nor is it an option that depends on a particular theological view about the role of a minister or priest, given the lack of consensus among those conducting weddings as to whether a minister or priest should themselves be authorized. Of the two Roman Catholic priests we spoke to, Dan appeared to have taken it for granted that he would be authorized, but John explained that he was not because the priest he had worked with preferred to keep the "roles of church and state" separate. Similarly, while Simon performed a dual role, he was quick to point out that there was no theological reason for him to do so, and that there were plenty of free churches in which it was not the minister who was authorized; as he added, "we certainly don't view that it has to be the priest or the minister who would need to be that person".

There did, however, appear to be a high level of awareness of the option of being authorized and of the necessary processes. Dan noted that when he was appointed as a Roman Catholic parish priest, he had "then registered as an authorized person with the ... registry office". Simon also seemed to have found the process straightforward, describing it as just a matter of completing the paperwork.

---

[46] Except in the case of different-belief marriages, for example that of David: see further Chapter 5.

There was also a structural factor that facilitated the presence of an authorized person at weddings in Christian places of worship. An authorized person is authorized to take responsibility for registering a wedding in *any* registered place of worship in the registration district of their own registered place of worship. Thus, for example, a Baptist authorized person may attend and take responsibility for registering a wedding in a Methodist registered place of worship within that registration district. With numerous Christian places of worship being registered, relatively similar marriage services, and a focus on ecumenical cooperation, it would be surprising if a Christian place of worship was not able to enlist the services of an authorized person if it so wished.[47] While as a matter of law, such cooperation may also extend across faiths – enabling that Baptist authorized person also to attend and take responsibility for registering a wedding in a registered mosque, gurdwara, or temple – the differences in belief mean that this is less likely to happen.

The invisibility of the prescribed words

As our discussion of Catholic weddings illustrated, how the prescribed words are experienced depends very much on how they are incorporated within the religious ceremony. There is a significant difference between weddings in which the prescribed words are identified as such and isolated from the rest of the ceremony and those in which the prescribed words are woven into the religious liturgy so that the join between the two is invisible.

When the Marriage Ceremony (Prescribed Words) Bill was being debated in Parliament, it was noted that the text of the new words had already been 'agreed by the Roman Catholic and Free Churches as being appropriate to the forms of their liturgies'.[48] In the modern liturgy of the Methodist Church, for example, the declarations are pared down to the question 'Are you, *AB*, free lawfully to marry *CD*?' and the answer 'I am', and so barely impinge on the ceremony. These declarations are separated from the words of consent by a combination of scripture readings, a sermon, and a hymn. The words of consent appear under the heading 'The vows'; the words that are prescribed by law are in bold type but otherwise appear as one with the rest of the 'solemn vow' made by each of the couple.[49]

---

[47] Such cooperation has a long history: see Rebecca Probert and Liz Harris (2021) 'Crossing the denominational divide: authorised persons and the registration of weddings in Desborough's Nonconformist chapels' 5 *Journal of Genealogy and Family History* 101.

[48] Hansard, HL Deb, 2 July 1996, Vol 573, col 1428 (Lord Bishop of Southwark).

[49] The Methodist Church Liturgy for the Marriage of Any Two Persons: www.methodist. org.uk/media/23099/marriage-of-two-persons-liturgy-approved-by-the-2021-confere nce.pdf

Similarly, within the modern Catholic 'Order of celebrating matrimony', the priest begins by putting certain questions to the couple about their willingness to marry and intentions for the marriage.[50] There then follows the 'Civil declaration of freedom', which is clearly designated within the liturgy as being required by law. The priest then invites the couple to declare their consent with the following words: 'Since it is your intention to enter the covenant of Holy Matrimony, join your right hands and declare your consent before God and his Church.' While that declaration of consent is made in accordance with the words prescribed by law, it segues seamlessly into 'to have and to hold from this day forward, for better, for worse, for richer, for poorer, in sickness and in health, to love and to cherish, till death do us part'.

The successful integration of the prescribed words was reflected in David's comment that the form of his ceremony was determined by the Catholic Church.[51] While he was aware of the fact that there were words prescribed by law, these words had not obtruded on the ceremony. The virtual invisibility of the prescribed words was also illustrated in Simon's reaction to the Law Commission's proposal that prescribed words would no longer be required in a religious ceremony. His concern was that he would no longer be able to require that the Baptist ceremony be used; for him, the prescribed words were those prescribed by his church, not by the state.

Recognizing religion

The experience of our participants suggests that descriptions of a wedding in a registered place of worship as 'civil' is ambiguous in meaning. While both Sam and David at times referred to the wedding in a place of worship as "civil", in context it appears that they simply meant that the religious ceremony had civil, or legal, effects. David, for example, noted that the Catholic ceremony "was also the civil ceremony", while Sam described his wedding as "a typical religious wedding".

Both Mary and David saw the wedding in a registered place of worship as a single ceremony that was recognized by the law, rather than as a religious ceremony with a separate 'civil' part. As Mary noted, "the legally binding ceremony is in the church". The fact that both ceremonies were Catholic was probably a coincidence; of more significance was the fact that an authorized

---

[50] 'Order of Celebrating Matrimony': www.liturgyoffice.org.uk/Resources/Marriage/OCM-Marriage-Texts.pdf

[51] It should be noted that David was somewhat critical of the priest who had conducted his wedding, as the latter made few concessions to the fact that David was not Catholic: see further Chapter 5.

person was in attendance at their respective weddings. By contrast, Sam, whose wedding was attended by a civil registrar, referred twice to the "legal element", once when alluding to the vows and once when trying to explain the difference in meaning of his two ceremonies.

Since the focus of our study was on couples who had had a non-legally binding ceremony, it cannot be taken as representative of the 10,000 or so couples who marry in a Christian registered place of worship each year.[52] But that background means that our sample is likely to over-represent those who had experience of different types of ceremony and so might be expected to be more attuned to what is required as a matter of religion and what is required as a matter of law. Sarah was aware of the prescribed words because they had constituted virtually the entirety of the pared-down wedding she had due to COVID-19 restrictions, but her general perception was that "as a Christian, I can have the type of service I want, ideally also legally recognized".

Conclusion

Our aim in this chapter has been to add some nuance to the debate about the way in which the marriage law engages with different religions and belief systems. It is important to appreciate the difference between making provision for weddings in a way that favours those conducted according to Christian rites and formally recognizing all Christian weddings. At different times, couples in many Christian groups have not been able to avail themselves of the option of getting married in a registered place of worship, and many Christians have experienced the prescribed words as a separate 'civil' ceremony. But it is equally important to appreciate the historical, legal, and structural factors that make it easier for legally recognized weddings to take place in places of worship registered by Christian groups and for Christian couples to believe that the law recognizes their religious ceremonies.

Those getting married in a registered place of worship are, however, a shrinking number. At the start of the 20th century, weddings in registered places of worship accounted for 17 per cent of all weddings, and while this fluctuated over the decades, the increase in the Catholic population brought the figure to 20 per cent in 1968.[53] By the close of the century, however, this had almost halved, and in 2019 just 4 per cent of weddings took place in places of worship registered by Christian groups.

---

[52] Office for National Statistics (2022) 'Marriages in England and Wales: 2019', Table 1. The figure cannot be stated exactly as Quaker marriages are included in the category of 'other Christian' marriages.

[53] See Office for National Statistics (2022).

That shift no doubt represents broader changes in religious allegiance.[54] But it is also likely to reflect changes in weddings in terms of the wider celebrations that accompany the ceremony. Mary's experience illustrated the challenges of trying to have a religious wedding and a celebration with family and friends: her choice of a small wedding in a church followed by a non-legally binding ceremony with a larger number of family and friends a few days later was influenced by her perception of "the stress" of getting everyone from the church to the venue and the lack of value in "paying all this money for basically a meal and a dance". Among our other interviewees, Phoebe had been considering having a ceremony in a Christian place of worship, but what she and her partner really wanted was to have an outdoor wedding.[55] Rather than assuming that the law works for Christian couples because it is (relatively) easy for them to get married in a registered place of worship, it should be recognized that the convention of getting married in a place of worship is an artefact of the law. There is, after all, nothing in the Christian theology of marriage that requires it to be celebrated in a particular place.

Under the Law Commission's recommendations, little will change for those Christian churches that already conduct weddings. They will be able to nominate officiants under the new scheme[56] and may, if they wish, require weddings to be celebrated in their place of worship, according to their own prescribed liturgy.[57] But they will also have the option of conducting weddings in a wider range of locations and will be able to choose to change their liturgy without needing to ensure that particular words are included.[58] That should make it easier – and possibly more attractive – for more Christian couples to have a wedding that reflects their beliefs. While Amanda favoured retaining prescribed words on the basis that "it would still be good to have certain wording that is the same, that just makes that legal part of it", she had perhaps not realized that these words are not prescribed for all under the current law.[59]

Moreover, in thinking about the extent to which the law currently respects beliefs in marriage, it is essential to understand that the apparent

---

[54] See Clive Field (2019) *Periodizing Secularization: Religious Allegiance and Attendance in Britain, 1880–1945* (Oxford University Press).

[55] See further Chapter 5.

[56] Law Commission (2022) *Celebrating Marriage: A New Weddings Law* (19 July), paras 4.256 (on the criteria that religious groups will need to fulfil in order to be able to nominate officiants) and 4.258 (on the transitional provisions that will apply to existing registered places of worship).

[57] Law Commission (2022), para 5.118.

[58] Law Commission (2022), para 5.78.

[59] See Chapter 2 on the different rules that apply to Anglican, Quaker, and Jewish weddings.

neutrality of the rules governing weddings in a registered place of worship is illusory. As we shall show in the next chapter, when the option of being registered was extended to non-Christian places of worship, no thought was given as to how different religious traditions might experience those rules.

4

Muslim, Hindu, Sikh, and Buddhist Weddings in Registered Places of Worship

'The way they deal with our ceremonies, where they're just not really anything, it's not really respectful to our culture'[1]

Introduction

In this chapter, we turn to the question of how the option of getting married in a registered place of worship works – or does not work – for couples in the four largest faiths after Christianity in England and Wales: Muslims, Hindus, Sikhs, and Buddhists.

This is an issue that has received surprisingly little attention to date. There is, of course, a substantial literature on how the legal requirements may pose challenges for different religious groups.[2] There is also a considerable body of empirical work examining ceremonies – primarily Muslim *nikah*s – that take place outside the legal framework in England and Wales.[3] What has

---

[1]   Arun, married on approved premises in a civil wedding followed by a Hindu wedding ceremony.

[2]   See, for example, Sebastian M. Poulter (1986) *English Law and Ethnic Minority Customs* (Butterworths); Anthony Bradney (1993) *Religions, Rights and Laws* (Leicester University Press); Carolyn Hamilton (1995) *Family, Law and Religion* (Sweet & Maxwell).

[3]   See, for example, Samia Bano (2012) *Muslim Women and Shari'ah Councils: Transcending the Boundaries of Community and Law* (Palgrave Macmillan); Rajnaara C. Akhtar (2015) 'Unregistered Muslim marriages: an emerging culture of celebrating rites and conceding rights' in Joanna Miles, Perveez Mody, and Rebecca Probert (eds) *Marriage Rites and Rights* (Hart Publishing); Vishal Vora (2016) 'The problem of unregistered Muslim marriage: questions and solutions' 46 *Family Law* 95; Kathryn O'Sullivan and Leyla Jackson (2017) 'Muslim marriage (non) recognition: implications and possible solutions' 39 *Journal of Social Welfare and Family Law* 22; Rajnaara C. Akhtar (2018) 'Modern traditions

been lacking to date is empirical work exploring how the legal requirements are perceived and experienced by different religious groups; this is what our study provides. As we will show, if the option of getting married in a registered place of worship is not seen as recognizing the parties' beliefs, then it is hardly surprising that couples might decide against this option and choose to separate the legal and the religious altogether.

In ascertaining the extent to which the law enables a couple to marry in accordance with their beliefs, it is particularly important to interrogate the claim that couples from non-Judeo-Christian groups need to have a 'civil' wedding in order to be legally married. Such claims may relate either to the perceived necessity of a separate wedding in a register office or on approved premises, or to the classification of a wedding in a registered place of worship as a civil one.[4] Here, it is significant to note that there are far more examples of this terminology being used in relation to non-Christian weddings than Christian ones.[5] In other words, 'civil' here usually denotes something more than the wedding being one that is legally recognized and conveys an important message about *what* is being recognized. As we will show, our participants almost invariably described weddings in non-Christian registered places of worship as involving a separate civil ceremony. The religious dimension to the ceremony was perceived to be legally irrelevant.

To show why the experience of marrying in a registered place of worship was so different from that of Christians, we first analyze how the legislative framework was not designed for non-Christian weddings, highlighting the absence of consideration given to such weddings in the debates over reforms to marriage law from the 1830s to the 1990s.

We then turn to examine how the option of getting married in a registered place of worship was experienced or perceived by Muslim, Hindu, Sikh, and Buddhist participants in our study. While relatively few had either married or conducted weddings in a registered place of worship, many had attended such weddings and had views on how they worked in practice.

---

in Muslim marriage practices, exploring English narratives' 7 *Oxford Journal of Law and Religion* 427; Islam Uddin (2018) 'Nikah-only marriages: causes, motivations, and their impact on dispute resolution and Islamic divorce proceedings in England and Wales' 7 *Oxford Journal of Law and Religion* 401; Rehana Parveen (2018) 'Religious-only marriages in the UK: legal positionings and Muslim women's experiences' 6 *Sociology of Islam* 316.

[4] See, for example, Home Office (2018) *The Independent Review into the Application of Sharia Law in England and Wales* Cm 9560 (Home Office), 17.

[5] See, for example, Ralph Grillo (2015) *Muslim Families, Politics and the Law: A Legal Industry in Multicultural Britain* (Ashgate), 45; Shaista Gohir (2016) *Information and Guidance on Muslim Marriage and Divorce in Britain* (Muslim Women's Network), 27. See also Norman Doe (2018) *Comparative Religious Law: Judaism, Christianity, Islam* (Cambridge University Press), 291, in which the terminology of 'civil marriage' is reserved for weddings taking place in mosques.

An option not designed for non-Christian weddings

As discussed in Chapter 3, the option of getting married in a registered place of worship was designed for Christian weddings. It was unsurprising that provision for non-Judeo-Christian faiths did not feature in the debates over how weddings law should be reformed in the 1830s given how few followers of such faiths lived in England and Wales at the time.[6] On the rare occasions that legislators acknowledged the existence of other faiths, they were referring to weddings taking place overseas rather than considering how weddings might be conducted in England and Wales.[7] Such discussion did at least lead some to consider the significance of having to marry in an unfamiliar and potentially alien form. One peer sought to create empathy for the plight of Unitarians who did not wish to invoke the Trinity by pointedly asking his fellow peers whether they 'would be satisfied with a marriage ceremony for themselves, in which the name of Mahomet was adjured'.[8] But the general perception was that adherents of other faiths were not 'sufficiently numerous' to require express provision to be made for them.[9]

Indeed, under the Marriage Act 1836, only places of Christian worship could be registered for weddings. This limitation was not explicit on the face of the legislation, but it was implicit in the fact that the building had to be 'certified according to Law as a place of Religious Worship', a possibility that was only open to Christian denominations at the time.[10] Although the Places of Worship Registration Act 1855 removed the limitation that only Christian places of worship could be certified as such, even into the 1890s we find legal commentators suggesting that 'a Mussulman mosque or a pagan temple could not be registered for marriages'.[11]

By that time, the question of how followers of non-Judeo-Christian faiths could marry had become a practical one. The Liverpool Muslim Institute

---

[6] For estimates, see G. Beckerlegge (1997) 'Followers of "Mohammed, Kalee and Dada Nanuk": the presence of Islam and South Asian religions in Victorian Britain' in John Wolfe (ed) *Religion in Victorian Britain: Vol V, Culture and Empire* (Manchester University Press); Rozina Visram (2002) *Asians in Britain: 400 Years of History* (Pluto Press); Humayun Ansari (2004) *The Infidel Within: Muslims in Britain since 1800* (Hurst); Sophie Gilliat-Ray (2010) *Muslims in Britain* (Cambridge University Press).

[7] See further Rebecca Probert (2023) 'Religious-only marriages in England and Wales: taking the long view' in Samia Bano (ed) *The Sharia Inquiry, Religious Practice and Muslim Family Law in Britain* (Routledge).

[8] Hansard, HL Deb, 2 April 1824, vol 11, col 84 (Earl of Harroby).

[9] Hansard, HL Deb, 3 June 1825, vol 13, col 1030 (Earl of Liverpool).

[10] Stephen Cretney (2003) *Family Law in the Twentieth Century: A History* (Oxford University Press), 35.

[11] William Nevill Montgomerie Geary (1892) *The Law of Marriage and Family Relations: A Manual of Practical Law* (Adam and Charles Black), 89.

had opened on Christmas Day 1889 and conducted its first (non-legally binding) marriage ceremony in April 1891.[12] Yet no mention was made of this development in the debates that led to the passage of the Marriage Act 1898, which allowed the authorities of registered places of worship to appoint their own authorized persons. Moreover, while nothing in the terms of the 1898 Act would have posed problems for a Muslim place of worship, it was interpreted in a way that precluded an authorized person being appointed by any non-Christian place of worship.[13]

While that particular anomaly was redressed by the Marriage Act 1949,[14] the fact that this was merely a consolidating measure meant that there was no opportunity to reconsider how it worked for the still-small but growing number of followers of non-Judeo-Christian faiths. If anyone had given it any thought,[15] the fact that two mosques had been registered for weddings[16] might have led them to assume that the framework was sufficiently flexible to accommodate any religious group without considering the implicit Anglican bias of the prescribed words.

The real problem was not that non-Judeo-Christian places of worship could not be registered for weddings, but rather the lack of such places to be registered.[17] It has been estimated that in 1961 there were 50,000 Muslims, 16,000 Sikhs, and 30,000 Hindus in England and Wales; while many informal places of worship may have existed, only seven mosques, three gurdwaras, and one mandir had been formally certified with the Registrar General and were eligible to be registered.[18] Of these, only three – all mosques – were actually registered for weddings.[19] As a result, any Hindu or Sikh couples and the majority of Muslim couples had to

---

[12] For the details, see Rebecca Probert (2021) *Tying the Knot: The Formation of Marriage 1836–2020* (Cambridge University Press), 126. While the institute was not the only mosque in England – another had opened in Woking a few months earlier – it was the only one conducting wedding ceremonies at that time.

[13] See Probert (2021), 160–1.

[14] See Probert (2021), 196.

[15] The committee appointed to consider the Bill that became the Marriage Act 1949 heard evidence from a variety of groups, but there was no discussion of the position of non-Judeo-Christian faiths.

[16] These were the Woking and East London mosques, registered in 1920 and 1943, respectively: Probert (2021), 188.

[17] For discussion of the challenges facing Hindus, Muslims, and Sikhs in either seeking to convert existing buildings or construct new ones, see Urfan Khaliq (2002) 'The accommodation and regulation of Islam and Muslim practices in English law' 6 *Ecclesiastical Law Journal* 332, 339–40.

[18] Ceri Peach and Richard Gale (2003) 'Muslims, Hindus and Sikhs in the new religious landscape of England' 93 *The Geographical Review* 469, 478.

[19] See Probert (2021), 201.

get married in their local register office, with any religious celebrations taking place separately. For that generation, separate ceremonies were the only option for those who wanted to be married in the eyes of the law and their faith.

Over the course of the 1960s, increasing immigration led to more places of worship opening and, in due course, being registered for weddings. By 1970 there were at least *some* places of worship in England and Wales in which Muslim, Hindu, Sikh, or Buddhist couples could marry.[20] But the fact that it was legally possible for couples from across the country to get married there[21] did not mean that it was practicable for them to do so. As a result, many still had to settle for having two ceremonies. Among our participants, Satnam, a Sikh priest, recalled that in 1978 when he got married, there was no "civil marriage" at the gurdwara so he married in a register office two weeks before his "actual wedding".

However, practices changed as more places of worship were certified and registered. As a result, when reforms to weddings law were discussed in the 1970s and 1980s, it may have been assumed that no consideration needed to be given to whether changes were needed to accommodate the practices of non-Christian groups. The removal of the condition that only a 'separate' place of worship could be registered for marriages provided an all too rare example of legislators noting that the change would benefit non-Christian faiths.[22] By contrast, in 1996 when the prescribed words were revised, no consideration was given to how these words were incorporated into non-Christian weddings.[23]

In short, the current law was not devised with non-Christian weddings in mind, and until relatively recently reformers have not considered whether more needs to be done to accommodate such weddings.

Before we consider how the option of getting married in a registered place of worship works (or does not work) for Muslims, Hindus, Sikhs, and Buddhists, we outline what constitutes a marriage within these different religious traditions so that readers can begin to see why the current legal requirements do not work well for these ceremonies.

---

[20] See Probert (2021), 203–4.

[21] Couples could marry in a place of worship outside their own registration district(s) if there was no registered place of worship in their own district(s) in which they could be married according to the forms, rites or ceremonies of their own denomination or faith: Marriage Act 1949, s 35.

[22] See Probert (2021), 226. This particular change was made by the Marriage (Registration of Buildings) Act 1990.

[23] Cf the express discussion of how they fitted with the liturgies of the Roman Catholic and Free Churches: see Chapter 3.

Muslim, Hindu, Sikh, and Buddhist weddings

Muslim weddings

The celebrations marking a *nikah* ceremony can differ significantly between different Muslim ethnic groups in England and Wales. However, its foundational pillars remain the same: a ceremony in which there is the verbal exchange of consent through an offer (*ijab*) and an acceptance of marriage (*qabul*), often (though not necessarily) presided over formally by an imam or other religious official.[24] The exchange of consent should be witnessed by two adults, and the *nikah* contract (usually written) is expected to make reference to *mahr*, a pre-agreed gift from the groom to the bride.[25] The *nikah* has significant spiritual connotations, being described as "an act of worship" by Ismail, an imam. There is a general consensus that the *nikah* should be "announced" (as mentioned by Ahmed), and therefore a public celebration, in which those gathered usually offer prayers for the couple and their future life together, is considered virtuous if not compulsory.

The simplicity of the ceremony was evident from the comments of multiple imams who described the ceremony itself as being short and offered little detail beyond 'doing' the *nikah*. Many took care to extend the performance of their role to include a longer sermon. The *nikah* sermon (*khutba-tun-nikah*) usually follows the *nikah* ceremony and often includes spiritual reminders about marriage and family. Some imams described taking a more personal role, whether by instilling humour through teasing the bride or groom, insisting the bride was present on the head table to sit with the groom and imam, or providing explanations of the process for guests, especially those who were not Muslim and required some context to the ceremony.

In some Muslim communities, there is gender separation at the time of the ceremony, and this may mean that the bride and groom are not together during the ceremony itself. Musa stated:

'Most of the times the *nikah* that take place, usually it's only men there. And there will be women, but on the other side … so basically we take the consent from the bride … before even the *nikah* ceremony is taking place. So, you go to the bride, take permission from them, and after that … you just do the *nikah* with the groom only.'

---

[24] In Muslim-minority jurisdictions where there tends to be no state oversight of the *nikah*, the role is usually performed by an imam or others attributed as 'knowledgeable' (of faith). In Muslim-majority jurisdictions, there is usually a legal process whereby state-sanctioned officials perform a legally recognized role, though the ceremony itself remains the same.

[25] Raffia Arshad (2010) *Islamic Family Law* (Sweet & Maxwell).

Ayman described a "gradual" move away from gender segregation, stating that it is "nothing to be squeamish about" to have the bride and groom sitting together.

The *nikah* celebration is usually followed at a later date by a wedding feast, often referred to as a *walima*, which is hosted by the groom's family. A few of our participants explained that the *nikah* meant they were able to spend time together alone, while the *walima* was their wedding, after which they began living together.

Hindu weddings

Marriage in Hinduism is quintessentially a fire ritual presided over by a Hindu priest versed in the sacred Vedic texts. Certain elements are accepted as being necessary if the ceremony is to be recognized as valid in religious terms: the kindling of a sacred fire (*havan*) around which the bride and groom walk a number of times; prayers (*puja*); and the priest's intoning of Sanskrit hymns from the Vedas.

While in India, the bride and groom make seven circuits of the sacred fire (known as the *saptapadi* ritual), it is more common for Hindus in England and Wales to walk four times around (known as the *mangal phere* ritual). As one Hindu priest, Dev, noted, "very rarely we'll get the seven rounds option. That's only the northeast part of India, people, when they get married, they use seven. The rest, most of us, we use four rounds".[26] The sevenfold ritual can instead be reflected in a couple's making seven marital vows to one another during the ceremony. The centrality of the sacred fire was reflected in the indignation that Hindu priests expressed in response to suggestions from venues that a tealight (which may better fit with the venues' insurance policies) would suffice. As Shikhar commented:

'I find them very offensive and I told them ... that if you are taking money from the couple to do a religious ceremony, then you must follow the religious ceremony to the letter. ... You manifest the Agni [fire deity] over there and the Agni has to start blazing properly to give the blessing to the couple by cooking the oblation into the fire, the sesame seeds and the barley, and the clarified butter ghee. The tealight just does not do this.'

---

[26] Another Hindu priest, Shikhar, suggested that 90 per cent of weddings involved four *pheras*, adding: "It's only the Gujaratis where you have a slightly different ceremony, where the Lohanas and the Shas had the girl going round for the three rounds and the Patels, Brahmins, and all the other Gujaratis have the boy going round for the first three rounds." He also explained that he had conducted wedding ceremonies for the Arya Samaj, a reform movement within Hinduism, "where they have requested for seven *pheras*".

While a Hindu wedding will always take place under a wedding canopy (*mandap*), the exact content of a wedding event is normally the result of negotiated agreement between the priest, the bride and groom, and their respective families. As Ajey explained:

> 'Obviously there's things that you have to do, the … going round the fire, and those are the important parts. And then some of the other things like the washing of the feet, for example, we didn't really agree with it. They say that the husband and the wife are the personifications of god – we didn't agree with that as such, so that was omitted … it didn't mean anything for us.'

On the day of the wedding, the groom's party arrives in a procession, followed by the bride's ceremonial arrival with male relatives. The couple sit facing one another in the *mandap* with an auspicious cloth (*antarpat*) hiding them from each other's sight until it is lowered. Flower garlands (*jai mala*) are exchanged. A single sacred thread (*mangal sutra*) might be hung around their necks, and their right hands are symbolically joined (*hasta milap*) and their clothing tied together (*ganth bandhan*) while prayers are said. The bride's father might offer her hand in marriage (*kanyadana*). Later in the ceremony, the groom hangs a bridal necklace (*mangalsutra*) around his wife's neck and places bright red sindoor powder along the parting of her hair. The married couple might feed each other sweetmeats (*kansar*). The union is given a blessing (*aashirwad*) by the priest, and the bride says goodbye to her family (*vidai*) before starting out on married life.

Sikh weddings

Marriage in Sikhism is understood to be more than simply the legal union of two persons. At its heart is the *anand karaj*,[27] seen as the spiritual joining together of a man and a woman, both Sikhs, in a relationship modelled on the ever closer love between an individual's eternal soul (*atman*) and the Supreme Soul of God, with husband and wife becoming 'a single soul in two bodies'.[28] As Satnam, a Sikh priest, explained, *anand karaj* could be

---

[27] While the *anand karaj* marks the point at which the couple are married within Sikhism, the process of getting married includes additional ceremonies and rituals such as a formal engagement (*kirmai*), the adornment of the bride with henna (*mehndi*), the formal meeting of the males of both families (*milni*), a breakfast for guests in the gurdwara's communal kitchen (*langar*), and the bride leaving her parental home, and arriving at her husband's home (*doli*).

[28] 'Sikh matrimonial conventions and ceremony' Article XVIII in *The Code of Sikh Conduct and Conventions*, p 27. The code, an English translation of the *Sikh Reht Maryada*, is

simply translated as the "ceremony of bliss", embedding spiritual values in the couple and their future children.

Key to the *anand karaj* is the presence of the Sikh holy text, the Sri Guru Granth Sahib. As a result, the ceremony will usually take place in a gurdwara, where its sanctity can be ensured. The ceremony itself can be performed by any Amritdhari Sikh (man or woman) who is able to recite the specified hymns and verses.

The ceremony commences with the reciting of a prayer (*ardaas*). The couple's parents stand, indicating their approval of the marriage. The bride and groom then kneel and bow their heads to touch the ground before the Sri Guru Granth Sahib. The bride's father places in her hands one end of the sash (*palla*) worn by the groom. The couple then walk four times around the Sri Guru Granth Sahib, each circuit accompanied by the singing of one of the four verses (*laavaan*) of a matrimonial hymn composed by the Guru Ram Das (1534–81), with the couple bowing their heads to the ground each time.[29] The ceremony is formally concluded with another prayer and the reading of a verse (a *vaak*) taken at random from the Sri Guru Granth Sahib, and then finally a sacred sweet halva (*karah parshad*) is distributed to the congregation.

Buddhist weddings

Buddhism considers marriage to be a secular concern and a matter of individual choice, and the specifics of a Buddhist wedding ceremony are a reflection of local cultural traditions rather than a prescribed liturgy or ritual. In England and Wales, communities following Buddhist traditions from Japan, Myanmar, Nepal, Sri Lanka, Taiwan, Thailand, Tibet, Vietnam, and other places are to be found practising and teaching, along with those following Western Buddhism or promoting meditation. More than a dozen of these communities have chosen to certify their place of worship as a venue for marriages, and their distinct cultural backgrounds have given rise to wedding ceremonies which are highly varied.

By way of illustration, the authorized persons for one particular Buddhist community described how weddings take place in front of their object of ritual devotion, a calligraphic scroll called the *gohonzon*. A typical ceremony starts with recitation of parts of the Lotus Sutra, followed by communal chanting of a mantra. The couple make solemn personal vows, and the

---

published by the Supreme Gurdwara Management Committee in Amritsar and is available at the committee's website: https://sgpc.net/?page_id=656

[29] For discussion of the religious significance of the *laavaan*, see Shinder S. Thandi (2016) 'What Is Sikh in a "Sikh wedding"? Text, ritual and performance in diaspora marriage practices' 23 *Journal of Punjab Studies* 131.

person conducting the wedding then declares them married in front of the *gohonzon* and in the presence of all the *bodhisattvas* of the Earth and of their friends and family. An address is given, celebrating the idea of partnership and explaining how the Buddhist faith will help the couple to overcome life's obstacles together. Because this particular community follows a form of Buddhism with its roots in Japan, the couple might choose to perform a version of the Japanese sake cup ceremony to symbolize their growing union. They might invite a friend to sing, read a poem, or contribute in some other way. The interviewees emphasized the importance of personalizing each wedding ceremony so that its content was tailored to each couple.

How the option of getting married in a registered place of worship works for Muslim, Hindu, Sikh, and Buddhist weddings

As discussed in Chapter 3, three factors determine whether and how the option of getting married in a registered place of worship works for any given religious group: whether the group meets the criteria to register its place of worship; whether it has specific requirements for a religiously recognized ceremony with which the prescribed words might conflict; and whether the ceremony is attended by a civil registrar or authorized person. As we will show in this section, these factors tended to operate in very different ways for Muslim, Hindu, Sikh, and Buddhist weddings.

In this section, we draw on the evidence from those who had married or had experience of conducting legal weddings in mosques, temples, gurdwaras, and a Buddhist centre. As noted in the introduction, relatively few of our interviewees had married in a registered place of worship. This was to be expected given how few legal weddings take place in Muslim, Hindu, Sikh, and Buddhist places of worship and given that we had set out to recruit couples who had had a non-legally binding ceremony. What was striking, however, was that none of these interviewees had a physically separate non-legally binding ceremony, held at a different time or place with a different celebrant;[30] rather, they generally conceptualized the religious wedding as itself consisting of two ceremonies, one civil and one religious. We also draw on the evidence from those who had had a non-legally binding Muslim, Hindu, or Sikh ceremony, to understand why they had chosen not to get married in a registered place of worship and how they perceived the option and, on the evidence from those who conducted such ceremonies, to understand the barriers to registration and authorization.

---

[30] Contrast those who had married in a Christian place of worship, who had all had an additional non-legally binding ceremony.

The limited number of registered places of worship

The lack of registered places of worship remains a key constraint. Across England and Wales, Muslim, Hindu, Sikh, and Buddhist places of worship are less likely to be registered for weddings than Christian ones, both in absolute terms and as a percentage of buildings that could be registered. Of 293 Sikh gurdwaras, 221, or 75.4 per cent, are now registered for weddings, but for Hindu temples, the percentage is just 42 per cent, with only 103 out of 245 being registered.[31] More mosques are registered for weddings in absolute terms, but as a percentage of the overall number of 1,443 mosques, 306 being registered for weddings is considerably lower in percentage terms, at just 21.2 per cent.[32] And Buddhists had both the smallest percentage and the smallest number registered, with just 14, or 12.2 per cent, of their places of worship registered for weddings.

Viewed as a percentage of actual places of worship, rather than those that have been formally certified as such, the disjunction is likely to be even greater.[33] When one factors in the theological, linguistic, and ethnic differences within different branches of Islam, Hinduism, Sikhism, and Buddhism, the likelihood of a couple being able to marry in the place where they worship is reduced still further.

As a result, there will be many registration districts in which couples have no place of worship in which they can legally marry in line with their beliefs. While the Marriage Act 1949 does allow for a wedding to take place in a different registration district in such cases, that will not always be practicable. For Muslims living in Cornwall, Devon, or Somerset, the closest registered mosques are in Bath and Bristol, while for those in Wales, the choice lies between Cardiff (which has four mosques registered for weddings) and Bangor (which has just one). But even discovering that information requires an awareness that there is an official list of all registered places of worship, and individuals are unlikely to find that list unless they are also familiar with the legal terminology.

---

[31] The figures here relate to the percentage of certified places of worship that are registered for weddings. There may of course be many places where groups meet for worship that are not certified as places of worship, but there are no official statistics for such places.

[32] There have been claims that the number of registered mosques is far higher. Amra Bone, for example, claimed that 1,360 mosques (which she estimated to be 69 per cent of all mosques) are registered (2020): 'Islamic marriage and divorce in the United Kingdom: the case for a new paradigm' 40 *Journal of Muslim Minority Affairs* 163, 166. However, that overlooks the all-important difference between being certified and being registered.

[33] Bone, for example, notes that there are an estimated 1,975 mosques in England and Wales, which suggests that almost a third are not certified as places of worship and so not eligible to be registered for weddings: (2020), 166.

Within our sample, some interviewees were aware of the option of getting married in a registered place of worship and had decided against it.[34] Others knew that it was a possibility in theory but did not regard it as an option in practice: as Karim commented, "very few mosques in the whole country actually have the registration process". And yet others were seemingly unaware that this was even a possibility. Adnan, for example, explained that an imam had advised them of the necessity for a separate legal wedding, although he added that he felt that there was "a bit of ambiguity" as to what was required. Similarly, Amal's comment that it would be "fantastic" if weddings conducted in a place of worship were to be recognized indicated that she was not aware that this was already an option.

Indeed, our findings suggest that a cultural assumption that there has to be two ceremonies means many couples do not even check to see if they can marry in a registered place of worship in the first place. Kiran noted that the mosque in her husband's town "do both the *nikah* and the civil ceremony ... you can do it in one shot, basically"; she added, however: "But I didn't know. The formality is that you have the *nikah* done where the girl lives." Similarly, when asked why she had chosen to have two separate ceremonies – a register office wedding in the morning and a *nikah* in a nearby mosque in the afternoon – Ada simply replied, "obviously, the *nikah* was non-legally binding, and I wanted to make sure that we had a contract which was recognized by law as well. And, unfortunately, we couldn't have the civil at the mosque and we couldn't have the *nikah* at the council".

It should be noted that the registration of a place of worship for weddings depends on an application being made by its trustees or governing authority. To that extent, registration is a choice, and there is evidence of some religious groups deliberately choosing not to register their places of worship.[35] However, a place of worship can only be registered for weddings with the support of 20 householders who use the building as their usual place of 'public' religious worship, and not all religious groups will be able to satisfy that requirement.[36] In addition, some individuals reported experiencing

[34] These included Miriam, who was in a religious-only marriage but noted that her imam told her "if you wanted your civil to be done at the same time, these are the other mosques you can go to", and Farid, who was also aware that some mosques offered this option.

[35] There was some suggestion in one focus group that the mistaken belief that they would be compelled to conduct same-sex weddings had deterred some mosques from being registered and led others to deregister, although it should be noted that the issue of non-registration long predates the introduction of same-sex marriage.

[36] For discussion of the challenges that may arise in showing that a particular place of religious worship is a 'public' one, see Rebecca Probert, Rajnaara C. Akhtar, and Sharon Blake (2022) *When is a Wedding not a Marriage? Exploring Non-legally Binding Ceremonies: Final Report* (Nuffield Foundation), 75–76.

challenges in registering their place of worship for weddings. One imam, Yousha, reported his frustration at the slowness of the process:

'We applied for registration of the centre last year and ... we're still here now ... 12 months later, with no paperwork and continuous headaches from them ... I don't know whether it's COVID or just the inability to be able to deal with an application. I don't understand what's going on between them.'

The difficulties in becoming authorized and the intrusive role of the registrar

An authorized person may be appointed for any registered place of worship, and within our study we spoke to a number of individuals who were, or had been, authorized. Idrees had been "one of the imams registered ... with the local council"; Uzair described the process for becoming an "authorized marriage conductor"; Sophea and Tara were both authorized persons at a Buddhist place of worship; and Satnam noted that "we have official people who can conduct civil weddings at the gurdwara".

However, not all of those involved in conducting ceremonies were aware of the option of being authorized. Lack of awareness was a particular theme among the imams: Musa said that he had tried to find out, but had only been able to find information on registering the building; Arif, Damal, and Xayd had not been aware of the option of being authorized prior to the interview; and Samir had similarly assumed that a registrar had to be present. Xayd also confirmed that none of the mosques with whom he was connected were aware of the option either, and Arif similarly thought that the vast majority of mosques across the country were unaware. As Xayd asked, "why [do] local authorities not make us aware so we can apply?"

In fact, none of the imams reported their local registration services proactively suggesting that they become authorized. This was in contrast to the experience of the two Buddhist authorized persons, Sophea and Tara. Indeed, Khalil felt that he was being subtly discouraged from applying:

'I found that system in order to apply and go through to be able to become an approved person is not transparent ... it's not something that I personally feel is welcomed by the councils. ... I contacted, I think it was a few years ago, the registrar office, and I wasn't given really satisfactory answers. I was asked to go onto a particular website and go through and read the requirements, etcetera. ... I don't know whether anybody else has felt that way, but I just feel that there isn't a concerted effort to incorporate approved personnel from other religions to be able to register a civil marriage.'

Jamal and Ismail also reported that they had not pursued the option of being authorized, with the former alluding to the "tonne of information" that the council had sent them and the latter commenting that the training required "too much involvement". The starkest evidence came from Ayman, who reported that his local register office had actually refused to accept him as an authorized person:

> 'We fulfil all the conditions. We've got a safe, proper safe. I know what I'm doing very clearly. I've done it a couple of times with the superintendents and, well, I conduct it all. But no … they said, "because you don't get enough … you don't get lots of people coming to you, that is one of the reasons why we're not giving the register to you people".'

As we noted in Chapter 3, the number of Christian registered places of worship and the extent of cooperation between different denominations means that registered places of worship without an authorized person will often be able to call on the services of an authorized person for a different place of worship. Crucially, however, this is only an option where both places of worship are within the same registration district. As Shikhar commented, the fact that it was only possible to be authorized for one particular area did not fit with the way in which Hindu priests travelled "all over the country, all over the world" to conduct wedding ceremonies.

As a result, it is reasonable to infer that a wedding in a Muslim, Hindu, Sikh, or Buddhist place of worship is more likely to be conducted in the presence of a registrar than one in a Christian place of worship. That, as Ayman noted, had practical implications for the couples who might wish to marry there: "That's again an off-putting factor for people to register there and then pay extra for the superintendent to come into the mosque and to do both the civil and the Islamic *nikah*."

The presence of a civil registrar is likely to be particularly unpalatable to those who accord a particular role to their own priests. One Hindu priest, Arjun, articulated a clear sense of a clash between spiritual and state authority; for him, the priest was the ultimate authority because he was responsible for "calling the gods" as witnesses to the marriage and "sanctifying that place", but then "somebody enters into that space with boots and all because of the health and safety restriction, whatever it is. And then they do something altogether different". A further source of tension was the fact that the registrar – rather than the priest – pronounced that the parties were husband and wife.

The prescribed words as a separate legal element

The inclusion of the prescribed words was regarded as particularly problematic by Hindu and Sikh participants. As discussed, within these religions it is the rituals that are performed that constitute the marriage. The bride and groom do not need to speak any words as part of the ceremony in order to become married. As a result, even having a requirement to say certain words, regardless of their content, can be seen as an alien imposition. Unsurprisingly, then, the prescribed words were not ones that had any cultural resonance for Hindu or Sikh couples. As Meera reported, when her sister married in a registered place of worship, she was told what to say and did not regard the words as meaningful in any way.

The inclusion of prescribed words was also seen as a disruption to the religious ceremony. As Dev, a Hindu priest, explained:

'It's dicing and splicing the Hindu wedding. It's getting disturbed. The ceremony is going on, we are doing, you know, *varmala* is happening, the garland exchange is happening, we are going to prepare for the *hastmelap* and religious ceremonies. And this ceremony is often put right bang in the middle of it, so we have to stop ... doing religious ceremonies and then this unknown person comes in as a registrar and he says, "Read the prescribed words and then I'll announce you as husband and wife". Then they walk away.'

Satnam used very similar terms to describe how he saw the prescribed words as disrupting the Sikh wedding ceremony:

'We have to have these official people who conduct these civil marriages in the presence of the congregation and at the Sikh wedding ceremony. It disrupts the Sikh wedding ceremony, and some people have it at the beginning, some people have it after. And some local authorities require us to have these civil weddings right ... bang in the middle of the Sikh wedding ceremony, which we are very, very uncomfortable about. Because it is like a spiritual thing that we have. It's a spiritual ceremony and we have like a secular ceremony getting in the way.'

That resentment of "these civil weddings" being "bang in the middle of" the religious ceremony shows how conflicting conceptions of the prescribed words may create difficulties. The Marriage Act 1949 does in fact direct that each party should make the required declaration and vow 'in some part of the ceremony'.[37] That is fundamental to the way that the option of getting married in a registered place of worship was conceived: the ceremony of the couple's choosing is given legal effect by the inclusion of the prescribed words. But if the prescribed words cannot easily be fitted into the rituals of

---

[37]   Marriage Act 1949, s 44(3).

a different religious tradition, it is easier for them to be said separately, and the common tendency to refer to a place of worship as being registered "for civil marriages" creates an assumption that there will be separate ceremonies.

Indeed, as Satnam went on to report, that had been the general practice within gurdwaras. Explaining that most "have got the facility where you can have the civil marriage at the gurdwara", he noted that these were initially conducted separate to the religious ceremony: "Either before or after. Normally after. So, we would have that spiritual wedding ceremony in one hall. Then after that was finished, we move onto another place where they would conduct the civil ceremony." However, this clear separation had since come to an end. As he explained, the "government" had "stepped in about two years ago" to inform them that "if you want to have civil marriage certificate, then it must be in the presence of the congregation at the religious wedding". He went on to say:

> 'So, we were very, very uncomfortable at that, but then we compromised that OK, after the wedding ceremony is finished, after the final prayer, that we will have the civil ceremony within the same congregation … the boy and girl will still be sitting together at the original place and they will go through the civil ceremony conducted by a separate officiant who'll get the signatures of the boy and the girl and the two witnesses in front of the congregation. We're not happy about that, but that is like a compromise that we have agreed to.'

Tara and Sophea similarly described how they had to make changes to the order of the Buddhist wedding in response to advice from their local register office that they were not allowed to write anything in the marriage register until the prescribed words had been said. The ceremony had originally begun with prayers and chanting but, as Sophea explained, they had "to completely turn [the] ceremony head on tail to be able to do the legal part at the very beginning to give the authorized person enough time, during the religious part of the ceremony, to do the paperwork". This led, as Tara confirmed, to a "mismatch" between the legal and religious aspects of the ceremony, with couples being legally married before the religious ceremony. She explained:

> 'So, we can't, in terms of our faith, declare them married, but they are legally married. So, it's like it's a bit of an awkward moment. It would just be much nicer to be able to focus on our religious ceremony, because that's why they're getting married with us, you know, because that's their faith and that's how they want to celebrate their union.'

While Benji, who had married in a Buddhist place of worship, was less negative about the prescribed words than many other interviewees, he was still conscious of them, explaining how the ceremony began with an introduction before "the legal declaratory words and vows were said" and then "interweaved back into the religious parts".

By contrast, Muslim participants expressed less antipathy to the prescribed words. This was in part due to the simplicity of the *nikah* ceremony, since its brevity meant that it was more difficult to disrupt, and in part to the fact that spoken vows were already part of the *nikah*.

Indeed, with no prescribed form for a *nikah*, the prescribed words could potentially be seen as a *nikah*. Karim noted that "Islamically, the moment that two people have accepted each other in front of witnesses, that's sufficient". Farah, whose legal wedding had taken place on approved premises, commented that "many people, even some Muslims, will say, well, this still amounts to a *nikah*", although she herself did not feel married at that point.

A few also commented on the similarities between the prescribed words and those used within the *nikah*. Farah had been struck by how similar the wording of her *nikah* was to that of her civil wedding, and Dania mused:

'It is just that the Islamic *nikah* has different terms. ... And even those, to be honest, like when you're listening to the vows or when you listen to them, they're the same. ... They are literally saying the same thing in whatever language. So, I think they're literally exactly the same thing, so just combine the two.'

However, in whatever way the prescribed words were incorporated into the process – whether they were carefully interwoven into the religious rites, perceived as a disruption, or said before or after other key words or rituals – they were always visible as a separate legal element. Unlike Christian participants, these participants were conscious that these were words prescribed by law rather than by their religion.

The importance of recognition
What is being recognized

As noted in the introduction to this chapter, the use of the term 'civil' to describe a wedding in a registered place of worship did not simply denote that the ceremony was one that was legally recognized, but also conveyed an important message about *what* was being recognized. For the majority of participants, the prescribed words constituted a "civil ceremony" within or alongside an unrecognized religious ceremony. Thus, Idrees regretted no longer being the authorized person for a mosque, noting, "I would have liked to continue helping couples by doing their Islamic and civil ceremonies in the same breath", and Rahil, a Hindu priest, referred to the "appointed assistant registrar" witnessing the religious ceremony and then coming up "to do the usual civil ceremony vows" with the couple.

It should be noted that not all participants appreciated the legal significance of the prescribed words: there was a common perception that it was the act of signing the register/certificate that constituted the marriage rather than the words spoken. Arun, for example, took the view that in the eyes of the law, "the registration is the thing that matters". Some found that idea difficult to reconcile with the prescribed words. As Vikram asked, "if the thing that binds you legally is a signature on a piece of paper, then why that certain language?"

However, that (mis)understanding tended to exacerbate rather than mitigate the sense that the law did not recognize their religious ceremonies. As Arun added, "for me, we got married when we completed our ceremony. We didn't get married when we signed a piece of paper". Meera similarly commented that "it's not just a piece of paper at the end of the day. It's a marriage". And Priya noted that had her ceremony been legally binding, "it would have been five minutes in a different room in a gurdwara, sign a piece of paper and it's just done. So, yeah, it doesn't really mean anything; anyone can sign a piece of paper".

What is not being recognized

The corollary of this was the clear sense among Muslim, Hindu, and Sikh participants that the law did not recognize their religious ceremonies.[38] Some commented on this directly. Priya, for example, thought that "it is a bit offensive to say 'well, you've been getting married like this for centuries and centuries but we've decided that we're not going to recognize it for whatever reason'". Darain expressed his understanding that "they don't formally recognize the *nikah* as a wedding ceremony as such", and Haris asked why the law did not recognize the practices of "major faiths" such as Islam.

Others noted that the position was different in other parts of the United Kingdom. Zahra thought that it was only in England that "your marriage isn't really accepted if you only have the *nikah*", commenting that in Scotland, where her sister had married, "you don't need to get the civil ceremony bit". While her perception that a *nikah* was recognized within Scottish law but not within English law somewhat exaggerated the differences between the two,[39] it illustrated how the presence or absence of certain requirements shapes how different options are seen.

---

[38] This sense was less marked among our Buddhist participants, whose ceremonies had taken place in the presence of an authorized person.

[39] In Scotland, couples still have to give notice before getting married, and any Muslim wedding must be attended by a celebrant who has been registered.

The sense of non-recognition emerged more obliquely when participants welcomed the Law Commission's proposed reform for England and Wales as ensuring legal recognition of their ceremonies. Jannat thought that the proposals would "support the recognition of a Muslim marriage", and Uma welcomed the idea of a Hindu ceremony being "legally recognized" if it "met whatever criteria the legal ceremony is required to meet".

To an extent, participants' perception that the existing law did not recognize their religious ceremonies was entirely accurate. There was, however, an underlying assumption that such non-recognition was not universal and that Christian weddings *were* recognized, although these ideas were often somewhat hazily expressed. Nadia, for example, referred to it being a "shame that *nikahs* are not viewed in the same way" in terms of being accorded legal recognition, and Salim spoke of his hope that the legal and religious could be amalgamated by having regulated imams undertaking marriages "just like a normal priest would in church". Dania alluded to the importance of recognizing "co-existing cultures"; similarly, Priya argued for "more cultural respect", commenting: "I don't know what the rules are when you get married in a church, but I think they're less stringent. I think you can do all of that in a church and it's all fine." Haris described the process as "obviously governed by" Christianity, while Adnan commented that "as long as all faiths would be treated equally in that it wouldn't be the case that a Catholic wedding or a Christian wedding has that status which other religions don't, then absolutely. As long as you get the chance to choose which one is the legal wedding, then that would make sense".[40]

The significance of recognition

In speaking of the importance of recognition, participants were not necessarily envisaging that a religious ceremony could be recognized in and of itself. Many spoke of the importance of having rigorous preliminaries and of regulating the person who would officiate at the wedding. As Haris noted, "I would say, you'd need to regulate that and you'd need to make sure that the right people are ordained". Kiran similarly thought it would be "awesome" if an imam was trained "to be a registrar".

But within that framework, the Law Commission's proposals were seen as marking a shift in the way that different religions were recognized. Shikhar welcomed the prospect of being able to "officiate and pronounce them as husband and wife, and make it as a legal binding wedding ceremony". For

---

[40] Adnan's mention of Catholicism reflected the fact that his wife was Catholic. On their chosen combination of ceremonies, see further Chapter 5.

many participants, the attractions of a single ceremony lay in the fact that it could, as Jane Mair has put it, 'satisfy legal and faith commitments in one cost-effective ceremony'.[41] Participants spoke of the greater ease of having a single ceremony and the savings in terms of both time and money.

A number also expressed the importance for a couple to be able to marry using the words that were meaningful to them. Some framed this in terms of the "sacred" element of marriage. Thus, Salim spoke of people from different religions currently not being allowed to use the words that they deemed sacred in their religious ceremonies, and Darain noted that "it's a sacred sacrament that you're taking". Others focused on the question of what was familiar, with Maryam commenting that "the idea of having something that ... comes naturally in your own ceremonies would be so much easier and it would actually give the sense of greater security, I think". Farah welcomed the idea that couples might be able to marry "in a way that's meaningful to them, what binds them together", her only caveat being that there would need to be clarity as to when a ceremony would be legally recognized.

There was also the broader question of how recognition would indicate greater respect for different religions. Again, many participants touched on this obliquely, referring to diversity and inclusivity.[42] Arun summed this up as follows: "It's the state and it's the law recognizing that the ceremony that you and your family and your partner and your culture respect and value is valued by the state and the law ... yeah, that's very welcome".

Conclusion

The prescribed words that fitted so seamlessly into the marriage services of Protestant Dissenters have understandably been seen as an additional – and perhaps unwanted – civil ceremony by faiths with their own rich traditions as to how marriages should be conducted. This sense of the prescribed words as a separate civil ceremony is even stronger when those words have to be repeated after a civil registrar, rather than an authorized person appointed by the place of worship. Exploring why the current law is perceived and experienced so differently by different faith groups is crucial to ensuring any future law operates fairly and with respect for different beliefs. This

---

[41] Jane Mair (2015) 'Belief in marriage' 5 *International Journal of the Jurisprudence of the Family* 63, 84.

[42] For examples, see Rebecca Probert, Rajnaara C. Akhtar and Sharon Blake (2021) *When Is a Wedding not a Marriage? Exploring Non-legally Binding Marriage Ceremonies: A Briefing Paper for the Law Commission*, paras 8.10–11, 8.29.

requires not simply having a common framework, but devising one that takes account of different religious traditions.[43]

Under the Law Commission's scheme, the ability to conduct legal weddings would no longer be limited to Muslim, Hindu, Sikh, or Buddhist groups that had registered their place of worship for weddings. At the same time, the flexibility of the current buildings-based system would remain in that there could still be multiple religious groups nominating their own officiants as long as each met the criteria to do so.[44] The new concept of the 'officiant' would also retain the flexibility of the old concept of 'authorized person': officiants would be tasked with ensuring that the requirements for a legal wedding are met, but need not be the person leading the ceremony (although they would be able to do so). In addition, religious weddings would no longer need to include prescribed words, with consent to the marriage being expressed 'by the parties' words or actions'.[45]

The case for reforming the law to allow for a marriage law that is no longer based directly on a Christian form of marriage is strengthened still further by the decline in adherence to Christian beliefs. Less than half of the population of England and Wales now profess themselves to be Christian[46] (and considerably less than half are likely to be practising). There is also an increased likelihood that a couple getting married will not share the same beliefs, and in the next chapter we turn to the particular constraints and challenges that this raises.

---

[43] Again, while our focus in this chapter has been on the particular challenges posed by the law of England and Wales, the issues raised have implications for other jurisdictions whose marriage laws were constructed around the practices of one particular religious group that no longer reflects the majority.

[44] Law Commission, *Celebrating Marriage*, para 4.256. See further Chapter 1.

[45] Law Commission, *Celebrating Marriage*, paras 5.78 and 5.118.

[46] Office for National Statistics (2022), 'Religion, England and Wales: Census 2021' (29 November).

5

Choices and Constraints
Where Couples Do Not Share
Religious Beliefs

'We felt that actually getting married in church may be a bit
one-sided'[1]

Introduction

So far, we have been discussing the options for couples to marry in a way that
reflects a particular belief. In this chapter, we turn to choices and constraints
that apply where couples do not share the same beliefs.

This is a topic that has received much less consideration in the scholarship
on marriage and religion.[2] Indeed, the topic of religious intermarriage in
England and Wales has received relatively little consideration among scholars
generally.[3] It was, however, a particularly salient issue within our sample,
since nearly a quarter of our interviewees did not share the same beliefs

---

[1]   Cyrus, explaining why he and his wife decided to have a civil wedding followed by two
      religious ceremonies.
[2]   The resource pack put together by the Inter-faith Marriage Network (see www.interfa
      ithmarriage.org.uk) helpfully includes a chapter on the options that are available, with a
      number of case studies, but this does not engage in analysis of couples' choices.
[3]   For commentary on the relative dearth of scholarship, see, for example, Jonathan Romain
      (1997) 'The effects of mixed-faith marriages on family life and identity' 28 *Journal of the
      Anthropological Society of Oxford* 275, 277, which referred to 'mixed-faith' marriages as 'a
      particularly striking, and as yet uncharted, phenomenon', and more recently Philip Sapiro
      (2020) 'Religious intermarriage in England and Wales: differences in individual and area
      characteristics of endogamous and exogamous couples' 36 *European Journal of Population*
      415, 415, which noted that religious intermarriage in England and Wales is under-
      researched 'when compared with ethnically divergent and immigrant/host intermarriage'.

as their partner.[4] In 10 cases, parties to the marriage could be classified as holding different religious beliefs, at least prior to the wedding,[5] while in a further 12 cases, one party held religious beliefs and the other described their beliefs as either agnostic or atheist, or did not have beliefs which they saw as fitting within a formal system of beliefs (often simply answering "none" when asked if they held any beliefs).

For the purposes of this chapter, we refer to these two groups as 'different-faith' and 'unshared-faith' couples, respectively. As we will show, it is important to distinguish between these two groups when considering how couples marry, since the constraints that apply to them, and the choices they make, are quite distinct. In addition to following what was legally possible or religiously permissible, different-faith couples wanted to ensure that their respective beliefs had equal weight and value in the process. The choices made by unshared-faith couples were largely determined by the religiosity of the party who held religious beliefs: if that person wanted a religious ceremony, the other generally went along with their wishes.

In this chapter, we first provide some context about the number of couples who do not share a belief and then go on to look at different-faith and unshared-faith groups in turn.

Context

Intermarriage in England and Wales does not have quite the same fraught history as it does elsewhere. The law has never prevented couples from different religious faiths from marrying each other. Nor, with the exception of Jewish and Quaker marriages, has it limited *how* they may marry, in contrast to jurisdictions where the religion of the parties determines the rules applicable to their marriage.[6]

That said, the options available to couples who do not share the same beliefs have often been somewhat limited, and attitudes have not always

---

[4]   For the purposes of this chapter, our focus is solely on religious beliefs. Helen, the only interviewee to specifically describe herself as Humanist, was married to someone who shared her beliefs: see further Chapter 7.

[5]   In addition to the five cases of different-faith weddings that we considered in the report, we also include here Simrat (Sikh/spiritual, Hindu husband), Priya (a Jain who converted to Sikhism upon marriage, Sikh husband), and Ajey, Dharval, and Vikram (all Jains with Hindu wives).

[6]   In 19th-century Ireland, for example, the validity of marriages between members of different denominations depended on how they were celebrated: see Rebecca Probert, Maebh Harding, and Brian Dempsey (2018) 'A uniform law of marriage? The 1868 Royal Commission reconsidered' 30 *Child and Family Law Quarterly* 217.

been positive.[7] Writing in the 1990s, Jonathan Romain alluded to the 'sense of public disgrace that had helped prevent many would-be mixed-faith marriages occurring' in earlier generations.[8] Even now, the advice and support provided for those in a relationship with someone who does not share their beliefs highlights the pastoral, societal, familial, and relationship issues that may arise.[9]

Generally, though, there is evidence that attitudes to marriages between persons of different faiths have become more accepting. When asked whether they would accept a family member marrying a person of a different faith, 74 per cent of respondents to the 2008 British Social Attitudes survey confirmed that they would 'definitely' or 'probably' do so; ten years later, this had risen to 82 per cent, with a remarkable rise, by 15 percentage points, in those who would 'definitely' accept such a marriage.[10]

However, estimating the actual number of couples who do not share the same beliefs is something of a challenge. Couples getting married make no statement as to their religious affiliation, and so researchers are dependent on decennial Census data for estimates. Drawing on data from the 2011 Census, David Voas has suggested that just 1.5 per cent of existing marriages involve spouses of different faiths, though the percentage is higher among younger generations.[11] By contrast, Sapiro's analysis of 359,000 'twenty-first century partnerships' found that 9 per cent were exogamous in that the reference person was married to a partner who did not share their beliefs.[12] The main reason for the difference between the two figures was that Sapiro, unlike Voas, had included Christians who were in a partnership with a person who had no religion. Excluding this group brought the percentage of exogamous relationships down to just 2.24 per cent.[13] The remaining difference can be accounted for by the fact that Voas' calculation included all couples living in a marriage with a person of a different faith, regardless of when that marriage formed, while Shapiro focused solely on those partnerships that

---

[7] See, for example, E.J. Trevelyan (1917) 'Marriages between English women and natives of British India' 17 *Journal of the Society of Comparative Legislation* 223.

[8] Romain (1997), 279.

[9] See, for example, Christian Muslim Forum (2012) *When Two Faiths Meet: Marriage, Family and Pastoral Care* (Christian Muslim Forum).

[10] David Voas and Steve Bruce (2019) 'Religion: identity, behaviour and belief over two decades' in John Curtice, Elizabeth Clery, Jane Perry, Miranda Phillips, and Nilufer Rahim (eds) *British Social Attitudes: The 36th Report* (Sage).

[11] David Voas, 'Religiously mixed marriages in England & Wales': https://dam.ukdataserv ice.ac.uk/media/604843/voas.pdf

[12] Sapiro (2020), Table 2. This sample was drawn from the Office for National Statistics' Longitudinal Study, which links Census data from 1971 to 2011 for individuals born on four specific dates.

[13] Calculated from the figures given in Sapiro (2020), Table 2.

had been formed in the 21st century. Shapiro's figures thus confirm Voas' suggestion that the percentage of marriages involving spouses of different faiths is higher among younger generations.

The high percentage of different-faith and unshared-faith couples within our sample reflected our focus on non-legally binding ceremonies; such couples were, in the absence of any express legal provision for an option whereby different beliefs could be combined, more likely than others to opt for such a ceremony. As we will show, however, among the unshared-faith couples it was not generally the lack of a shared belief that led them to choose a non-legally binding ceremony.

Our sample also illustrated the difficulty of determining when a couple should be classified as different-faith: Arjun described himself as part of a "mixed" couple on the basis that while his wife was also Jain, she identified more with Hinduism; meanwhile, Vikram and Dharval – both Jains married to Hindus – emphasized the common ground between the two faiths.[14] In this chapter, we have focused on those interviewees whose lack of a shared faith influenced the choices they made about how to marry.

Different-faith couples

Different-faith couples generally need to make a choice about whether their legal wedding will reflect the beliefs of just one of them or neither of them. In this section, we look first at the legal options that are available to these couples, reviewing the direct and indirect limitations on intermarriage and on the content of different forms of weddings. We then go on to consider the choices made by our interviewees in the light of these constraints.

Restrictions on intermarriage

There are two ways in which the law limits the options that are available to different-faith couples.

The first relates specifically to Jewish weddings. The special provisions that apply to such weddings are only applicable if *both* parties are regarded as professing the Jewish religion.[15] As discussed in Chapter 2, this had an impact on the choices available to David, who was marrying a Roman Catholic.

---

[14] Vikram emphasized the similarities between Jainism and Hinduism, and Dharval described Jainism as "an offshoot of Hinduism". For present purposes, the key point is that any differences between them did not affect their choice of ceremony. While Dharval noted that for him and his wife, "having a religious ceremony fused with the registered marriage ... could be complicated" because of differences between their Hindu and Jain backgrounds, he also described his religious ceremony as "Hindu–Jain".

[15] Marriage Act 1949, s 26(1)(d); see further Chapter 2.

Since getting married according to Jewish usages was not an option, their legal wedding took place in a Catholic church.[16] What he had not expected was that his Liberal synagogue would not be willing to conduct a non-legally binding ceremony for them:

> 'They had taken, in my view, an entirely unjustifiable and quite offensive decision that they weren't going to conduct weddings which were not capable of being legally binding. Which means, of course, not between two Jews ... I found the whole thing rather hurtful and I've never quite recovered I don't think, because although I was always very committed, I felt like because I wanted to have a wedding with, you know, somebody who wasn't Jewish, the synagogue and the rabbi there was just washing her hands of it.'

While he had found a rabbi who conducted ceremonies for people who "have fallen outside what is offered by mainstream Judaism", this was not what he had wanted:

> 'I mean, it's difficult because he was an incredibly nice man. Incredibly nice. I was carrying a lot of hurt from how I felt my synagogue had treated me. And so it wasn't quite the sort of thing that I wanted, because really what I had wanted was something whereby the Jewish bit was not only Jewish but also part of my synagogue, because that was really important to me.'

The second way the law limits options for different-faith couples is more indirect. Getting married in a registered place of worship is subject to the permission of its trustees or governing authority. If they wish to restrict weddings in that place of worship to couples of the same faith, they may do so.

Within Islam, the orthodox view is that a Muslim man may marry a non-Muslim woman from among the "People of the Book" – that is, Jewish or Christian – but a Muslim woman may not marry a non-Muslim man.[17] As a result, some imams would not conduct a *nikah* for a couple where the bride

---

[16] There are also legal restrictions on who may have a Quaker wedding, although these give the Society of Friends considerable discretion to allow non-Quakers to marry according to Quaker usages: Marriage Act 1949, s 47. On the evolution of the provisions relating to Quaker weddings, see Rebecca Probert (2021) *Tying the Knot: The Formation of Marriage 1836–2020* (Cambridge University Press), ch 4.

[17] See, for example, Mai Yamani (1998) 'Cross-cultural marriage within Islam: ideals and reality' in Rosemary Breger and Rosanna Hill (eds) *Cross-cultural Marriage: Identity and Choice* (Routledge).

was Muslim and the groom was not. Sikhism similarly places restrictions on marriage to a non-Sikh.[18]

Priya and Simrat had both faced obstacles in getting married. Priya converted from Jainism to Sikhism in order to marry her Sikh partner, but still struggled to find a gurdwara willing to conduct the ceremony. As she explained: "So, typically in gurdwaras you can't get married there unless your middle name or your surname was Kaur as a woman, to show that you are Sikh. And obviously I wasn't Sikh before we got married. So, even finding the gurdwara in the first place was really difficult." Having "called around 15 places", she eventually found one that was willing to conduct the wedding, although she had to sign a declaration "stipulating that my name would change to Kaur after we got married … and that I would raise my kids in the Sikh faith".[19] Simrat, who also wanted a Sikh ceremony, had experienced the converse situation: she had been baptized as a Sikh, but because she was marrying a Hindu, she knew it would not be an option for her:

> 'I always knew that in my religion that we wouldn't be able to have a Sikh ceremony because of my partner's name. Obviously, he is not a born Sikh, so he would not have Singh or Kaur in his middle name. So, I always knew that this was going to be a factor.'

When combined with the rules on where couples can marry, the power to prevent a marriage taking place in a particular registered place of worship may effectively deny different-faith couples the option of being married in a place of worship at all. In brief, couples are generally limited to getting married in a registered place of worship in their district of residence. The main exception to this rule – which allows a couple to marry in a registered place of worship in a registration district in which neither of them resides if it is the nearest one that solemnizes marriages according to the rites of the religious group to which at least one of them belongs[20] – does not cover the situation where a couple have been refused permission to marry. The other exception – which allows a couple to marry in a registered place of

---

[18]   'Sikh Matrimonial Conventions and Ceremony' Article XVIII in *The Code of Sikh Conduct and Conventions*, pp 26, 29. For the controversy attaching to the solemnizing of marriages in gurdwaras where one of the partners is not Sikh see *Eastern Eye* (2015) '"Thugs" ruin inter-faith wedding', 21 August.

[19]   In the event, the wedding had not gone ahead in this particular gurdwara on account of the COVID-19 regulations in place at the time: see Rebecca Probert, Rajnaara C. Akhtar, Sharon Blake, and Stephanie Pywell (2022) *The Impact of Covid-19 on Legal Weddings and Non-legally Binding Ceremonies*, 22.

[20]   Marriage Act 1949, s 35(1).

worship in a registration district in which neither of them resides if it is the usual place of worship of at least one of them[21] – will only offer a solution if it is practicable for one of the parties to make that place their usual place of worship. Otherwise, the only option is for one party to establish a temporary residence in a registration district that does contain a place of worship that accommodates different-faith couples.[22] This, however, is hardly a convenient (or cheap) option.

Restrictions on the options available to different-faith couples

Each of the options available to different-faith couples is also subject to restrictions, both direct and indirect, on the content of the wedding.

First, while a civil wedding is open to those of all beliefs or none, it cannot include any religious service or, if it is on approved premises, any material that is 'religious in nature'.[23] As a result, if a different-faith couple choose this option, their wedding will not be able to reflect the beliefs of either of them.

If the civil wedding is conducted on approved premises, there may be scope for the couple to have an additional ceremony or ceremonies reflecting their beliefs, although there will need to be a clear demarcation between the legal wedding and any additional ceremony.[24] For Cyrus, the transition between the civil wedding and his religious ceremony had been relatively seamless, with the latter taking place in the same room as the former: "Everybody sat still and we just switched over down the front, moved the table away, and proceeded with my religious element".

Second, it is generally accepted that Anglican clergy have an obligation to conduct the wedding of a couple who qualify to be married in their parish, regardless of the beliefs of the parties. This means that Anglican clergy, unlike the governing authorities of registered places of worship, do not have the right to refuse to marry couples unless a statutory exception applies.

---

[21] Marriage Act 1949, s 35(2).

[22] Under the current law, each party must give notice in the registration district in which they have been resident for the previous seven days: Marriage Act 1949, s 27(1).

[23] Marriage Act 1949, ss 45(2) and 46B(4); The Marriages and Civil Partnerships (Approved Premises) Regulations 2005, SI 2005/3168, Sch 2, para 11(2). On the interpretation of this requirement, see Stephanie Pywell and Rebecca Probert (2018) 'Neither sacred nor profane: the permitted content of civil marriage ceremonies' 30 *Child and Family Law Quarterly* 415.

[24] The guidance from the General Register Office is that the two ceremonies should be kept separate. For discussion, see Rebecca Probert and Shabana Saleem (2018) 'The legal treatment of Islamic marriage ceremonies' 7 *Oxford Journal of Law and Religion* 376. The requirement for the two to be separate was also an issue raised by the two interfaith ministers in our sample, Crystal and Stella, who discussed the possibility of having an additional interfaith ceremony on approved premises alongside a civil wedding.

However, while an Anglican wedding may be available to all regardless of their beliefs, it is less flexible in terms of its content than a wedding in a registered place of worship. As previously discussed, weddings in Anglican churches must take place according to one of the authorized rites of the Church of England or the Church in Wales.[25] Where rings are exchanged, each party is directed to conclude their promise to the other with the words 'in the Name of the Father, and of the Son, and of the Holy Ghost'.[26] The explicitly Trinitarian language will be a particular issue for Muslims, who recognize Jesus as a prophet but not as God.[27] In short, the possibility of being married in an Anglican church may be unattractive if the ceremony is at odds with the beliefs of one of the parties in a different-faith couple.

That said, there is some flexibility as regards the additional content. The Church of England's guidance for different-faith couples is that 'with the advice of the vicar, there may be places where you can bring an element of other traditions, cultures and even different languages into your service, perhaps through readings and music'.[28] Anna commented that her church had been very positive about her Hindu ceremony, and she praised the way in which the vicar had made a point of discussing it during the service: "She went out of her way to talk about that, which was really lovely and I think really meant a lot to [my husband's] parents". Fariha was equally positive about the Church of England vicar who had conducted her wedding and had even suggested having a reading from the Koran as one of the optional readings: "This was his first interfaith ceremony to conduct so he was ... I think he was quite nervous, but I also think he was quite excited about it. He really tried hard ... he wanted to have both faiths involved, which was really nice." However, such flexibility has its limits. While Fariha had not asked the vicar about the possibility of the *nikah* being conducted in the church, it is unlikely that this would have been permitted.

Third, if the governing authority of a registered place of worship is willing to host a wedding for a different-faith couple, there is, in principle, considerable flexibility as to the form that this ceremony can take, but in practice, it will depend on what the authority or the person conducting the ceremony will permit. David's perception was that "a feature of Catholicism

---

[25] See Chapter 2.

[26] This form of words is common to all three approved rites.

[27] Christian Muslim Forum (2012) *When Two Faiths Meet: Marriage, Family and Pastoral Care* (Christian Muslim Forum), noted that to avoid invoking the Trinity, one different-faith couple decided to have a blessing rather than a wedding.

[28] The Church of England, 'Mixed faith marriages': www.yourchurchwedding.org/article/mixed-faith-marriages/. For a recent example, see 'Life and love in mixed-faith marriages', *Church Times*, (2021) 2 July, which described a wedding at St Paul's Cathedral involving a Christian bride and a Muslim groom that incorporated Bengali poetry.

is one doesn't really get very much choice" and that his ceremony was "the standard service which they performed for a wedding between a Catholic and a non-Catholic". Having Jewish beliefs, David had specifically asked the priest conducting the Catholic ceremony (chosen to reflect his wife's beliefs) to leave out the promise to raise their children as Catholic and was upset that this flexibility was lacking: "It was like he couldn't even bring himself just to, you know, diverge from the liturgy by that tiny amount, you know." By contrast, Rupal, a Hindu priestess, noted that in cases of different-faith couples she would always do a "tailor-made service, exactly what they want and they decide". The two interfaith ministers in our sample, Crystal and Stella, also spoke of the possibility of a registered place of worship allowing them to conduct the wedding.[29] But as the latter noted, "the trouble is that we can legally marry people in places of worship, but the places of worship won't let us in".

In short, while the law does not restrict different-faith couples from marrying, it does not provide any guaranteed means by which they can do so in a way that reflects the parties' respective beliefs. The only form of wedding that has the potential to include more than an element of another faith's ceremony is one in a registered place of worship. Whether that is an option in practice is contingent on there being a place of worship that will permit this and on the couple being eligible to marry there.

Trying to ensure equal respect for beliefs: choices made by different-faith couples

In explaining the choices that he had made as to a combination of ceremonies, Cyrus spoke of how it was important that his beliefs were given equal weight and respect to those of his wife:

'I'm Zoroastrian, my wife is Christian. And ... her religion has the same sort of impact on her life as it does on mine. So she doesn't go to church every Sunday or anything. But she does identify as a Christian. ... Well, we had to do civil or get married in church. And we felt that actually getting married in church may be a bit one-sided towards [my wife's] side. So we thought well, actually, we would like something from my side, so then we finally decided, well, actually, what we will do is start with a civil ceremony, and do the legal bit, and then ... follow it immediately with a blessing from both of our

---

[29] Crystal had experience of conducting weddings in a registered place of worship, while Stella was aware of interfaith ministers having been allowed to conduct weddings in Unitarian churches and Pagan Goddess temples: see further Chapter 6.

religions. So what we did was we did the civil first, got it done with, then had [the priest] do our blessing, a Zoroastrian blessing, around 20 minutes or whatever. Thankfully, we were able to do it in the same location, all of that, straight after, literally. And then we were lucky enough to be married in a place where the church was literally just a short walk down the road.'

Anna's choice of a Christian wedding and a Hindu ceremony was similarly influenced by considerations of equality, although it created something of a dilemma for her:

'So, my first wedding was a church wedding, with my first marriage. And then I felt absolutely awful about being divorced really. It wasn't really what I believed in. So, when we were getting married again … the idea of another church wedding was just horrible for me. I just felt like I shouldn't be doing that. It was awful. And what we were looking at doing was a civil ceremony for the English side and then the full Hindu wedding. And we sort of started down that planning route and then … but then I felt it was becoming much more about his family and his side and less about mine.'

Tellingly, neither Cyrus nor Anna considered the option of getting married in a registered place of worship, their assumption being that the only available options for the legal wedding were either a civil wedding or a Church of England ceremony. As the former noted, "it seems it's a very limited option of getting married in this country. It's either a church or a civil, and there's no recognition of other religious ceremonies, as far as I'm aware, or at least not of Zoroastrian marriage ceremonies".[30]

Fariha was the only one who had specifically investigated the possibility of getting married in a registered place of worship, but she had struggled to find any information: "I found out on the … council website where all the licensed venues were and where all the churches were, but there was no database for any other faith, let alone the Muslim faith." This was not an administrative oversight: there was in fact no mosque registered for weddings in her registration district, or indeed within a 50-mile radius of her home.

Unsurprisingly, then, these interviewees had a strong perception that the current laws were profoundly *un*equal in how they accommodated different beliefs. Fariha commented that she felt it was "really unfair" that she could

---

[30] There is in fact one Zoroastrian place of worship that is registered for weddings, in Harrow: see UK Government, 'Places of worship registered for marriage': www.gov.uk/government/publications/places-of-worship-registered-for-marriage

not use her *nikah* ceremony "to become legally binded". Anna similarly expressed the view that it wasn't right "that a church wedding can be a legal ceremony and none of the other religions can". As she added:

'It's quite shocking that they haven't reformed it over the last ten years really, because … we're such a multicultural society now, and so it's quite sad really. That's just another thing that just adds to the fact that there is that tier system in this country where people still think there are different classes of people and some are better than others, or more worthy or more normal or more British.'

They navigated this clash between their desire for equality and the inequality of the options that were available to them by minimizing the differences between their different ceremonies. One strategy was to hold the legally recognized religious wedding as close as possible to the non-legally binding ceremony. The shortest gap was that experienced by Fariha and Felix. They had initially planned to have an hour's gap between their *nikah* ceremony and their Anglican wedding; in the event, the *nikah* ceremony started late and the gap was reduced to the single minute that it took to walk between the two locations. As Fariha reflected, in hindsight this had been a positive in helping to reinforce the sense of unity between the two ceremonies, as "they blurred into one another". Anna, meanwhile, explained why her Christian wedding and Hindu ceremony were not held on the same day:

'We did start trying to look at doing it in one day … but the vicar was quite funny about the earliest time we could have the wedding. So that scuppered those plans, which was a good thing in the end because I think it would have been a nightmare. So, we did decide to do it in one weekend. And we had the church wedding on a Saturday and the Hindu wedding on the Sunday. But that was purely because you don't really have church weddings on a Sunday. So we didn't have to think which one we were going to do first. And there wasn't really any conflict … I can imagine without that precedent, there might have been from our families' sides, "why was that one first?" But because it was easy to say "churches don't really do weddings on a Sunday, whereas Hindu weddings …", there was no problem with it being on a Sunday. That made that decision easy.'

She was conscious that any more significant lapse of time between the wedding and a further religious ceremony might send a message that the latter held no real significance. Referring to the six-month gap between two ceremonies of a relative, she commented "that really was a statement" that the second ceremony was not important, "especially as they acted like they were married after the first one". In a similar vein, David noted the risk that if a wedding was followed by a blessing at a later date, the "second bit" might be regarded as less important, whereas holding the two as close together as possible enabled them to be seen as forming part of a single whole.

A second way interviewees tried to minimize the significance of one of the ceremonies having legal effect was by focusing on the religious significance of both ceremonies. This was the case both where the legal wedding reflected their own religious beliefs and where it did not. As Anna explained:

'I don't think we ever actually really discussed the fact that the Christian wedding was the legal one and the Hindu wasn't. Because, actually, I think for both of us the religious part was more important and doing both of them was important. And then the fact that we could say "tick, we've done the legal side, we don't have to worry about an extra ceremony" was just convenient really. So, yeah, that was handy because having to have done three would have been difficult.'

Similarly, Fariha commented that "the Christian ceremony happened to be the legally binding one", later adding, "the whole legal aspect of the actual thing never really entered my mind, because I think for me it was about actually having those ceremonies and having it in front of our friends and family. That was the meaningful part to me".

Third, when asked which of the ceremonies had been the most meaningful, no one singled out the ceremony that reflected their own beliefs. Instead they emphasized how both (or all) of the ceremonies had been equally meaningful or even highlighted how the ceremony for their partners' faith had been more meaningful to them. Thus, Cyrus thought that "it wouldn't be fair" to single out one as being more meaningful than the others. Fariha had expected that she would find the *nikah* more meaningful, but on the day she had not been conscious of a difference between it and the subsequent Christian wedding, commenting of the latter: "I felt like I was getting married, obviously again, but I actually felt that, and I didn't think I would." And Anna came away from her "absolutely beautiful" Hindu ceremony "thinking that meant more to me than the Christian one".

Trying to ensure acceptance of different beliefs: familial considerations

The choices made by different-faith couples were about respecting not just each other's beliefs but also the beliefs of their respective families. For Parmita, who had eloped to Scotland to get married in a civil wedding with only two witnesses present, the two religious ceremonies that took place three years later were "less about religion" and "more about two families coming together"; she recognized that the (to her) unfamiliar Christian ceremony was important to her husband's side of the family and described it as a means of getting their blessing on the marriage. Cyrus similarly referred to wanting the process to be fair not only for he and his wife as a couple but also for their families' sakes, and Anna noted that having two ceremonies "was all about pleasing our families really".

Fariha also emphasized the importance to her parents of her having a *nikah*. At the same time, she and Felix had wanted to use the wedding to challenge her family's beliefs. As she explained, there had been a certain degree of pressure on Felix to convert to Islam. While her parents had eventually conceded that this was not necessary, she had ideally wanted a single interfaith ceremony.

The importance of getting married in accordance with one's beliefs

The fact that different-faith couples had experienced more than one form of ceremony meant that they were particularly conscious of the differences in the ways that marriage vows were framed in different faiths. Anna and Parmita spoke of how they had struggled with the ceremony that was not familiar to them. As a Hindu, the Christian blessing was unfamiliar to Parmita and made her feel nervous: "I felt that I'm not part of this tradition and very much imposter syndrome coming in." Conversely, as a Christian who had never attended a non-Christian religious wedding, Anna recalled: "I didn't know what to expect. I didn't know what it was going to look like, I didn't know what was going to happen, and I just had to go along with it really."

As Cyrus explained, marriage vows were not just a means of getting married but also a way of expressing beliefs:

> 'We thought perhaps we wanted to be married under vows that we are both comfortable with ... I don't know if it's the same for Christianity, but under the vows of Zoroastrianism, you ... vow to display certain values and traits, and perhaps even your commitment to our God and Prophet. And likewise I would suspect that a Christian wedding would commit that person to live under vows and, you know, and ... keep their commitments to a Christian God or Jesus.'

Similarly, the experience of having at least one non-legally binding ceremony made some conscious of the difference between a wedding and a blessing. Cyrus noted how having a prior civil wedding had affected the form of his subsequent Zoroastrian ceremony, saying it "wouldn't be right" to have the same vows and declarations that would normally form part of the religious ceremony once they were already married, "because, you know, it's a bit of hypocrisy if you've already got married, and you're still asking them 'are you ... ?'"

Equal but separate

When asked whether they would have wanted an option whereby both religious ceremonies could be combined, Fariha and Felix were particularly enthusiastic about the idea, as their ideal ceremony would have been jointly led by an imam and a Christian minister. Similarly, Cyrus was attracted by the idea of "something in between that would accommodate both our religions" rather than having to "do the civil".

By contrast, Anna expressed the view that different-faith marriages were not about "mixing" faiths, but rather having the two "standing alongside each other"; in her view, having a joint ceremony "would have ruined both sides". Even if it had been possible to have a combined ceremony, she would still have opted for separate ones.

If the ceremonies were to be separate, interviewees wanted either one to have the potential to be legally binding. David would also have liked his Jewish ceremony to be recorded alongside his Catholic wedding, with the marriage certificate including both locations and being signed by the rabbi as well as the priest.

Unshared faiths: accommodating beliefs and lack of belief

Similar choices face couples where one person holds religious beliefs and the other does not: whether to marry in a civil wedding without explicitly religious content (and if so, whether to have an additional non-legally binding religious ceremony) or in a religious wedding whose content assumes beliefs that one of them does not share.

Defining belief and lack of belief

Within our sample, we classified 12 interviewees as being part of unshared-faith couples.[31] These couples included different combinations and levels of belief and non-belief. Some reported straightforward parameters: Jane was Bahá'í and her partner was atheist. By contrast, Phoebe more tentatively described herself as "probably closest to Church of England" but "non-practising", and her husband as "more a spiritual believer", and Ellis, whose

---

[31] We did not include cases where an interviewee reported that their spouse did not fully share their faith: as Romain (1997) has commented, if different backgrounds or levels of religiosity are taken into account, then virtually every marriage could be regarded as being mixed-faith. We also excluded Arun despite his description of himself as "maybe" an "agnostic Hindu", as he made it clear that he subscribed "to the fundamental meaning of the religion".

wife, Emma, described herself as "not religious", explained how they were "raised Christian" and now had "a faith rather than a religion".

These 12 couples also had different levels and combinations of attendance at religious services and practice. Indeed, some atheists were more regular in their attendance than some who held very strong religious beliefs. Rhoda's atheist spouse, for example, was a bell-ringer at their local church and attended services there with her. Jay was initially the most vehement about his lack of religious belief, describing himself as "probably quite anti religion if anything"; however, he also acknowledged that he was "highly accepting" and happy to take part in festivals such as Diwali – or indeed Christmas and Easter.

As we have emphasized throughout, our sample was not intended to be representative. Given that the criterion for interviewees to be included in the project was having had a non-legally binding ceremony, these 12 couples are likely to be a very particular subset of unshared-faith couples: those who choose not to have a religious wedding but want something in addition to a civil wedding. Perhaps surprisingly, though, the fact that one partner had no religious beliefs was not generally the reason for these couples choosing not to have a religious wedding.

The reasons for not having a religious wedding

The only case in which the lack of a shared faith had specifically influenced the decision not to have a religious wedding was that of Phoebe. While her husband would have been happy to have a church wedding, she recognized that there would be an asymmetry in the ceremony: "Because I knew [he] doesn't wholly share my beliefs – he understands them and he's like 'that's your thing, sweetheart, whatever' – I didn't want to make him uncomfortable, making vows and promises in a way that he didn't wholly believe in, and that wasn't fair."

Even in this case, though, the lack of a shared faith was not the only factor. As Phoebe explained, although she had been a regular churchgoer as a child and her Christian faith remained important to her, she had stopped going to church as an adult because she couldn't find "the right fit of community" when she moved away from her childhood home. As a result, although the couple had considered a church wedding and even gone to different local churches, she had felt "this isn't quite right. This isn't quite what I want".

In other cases, unshared-faith couples chose not to have a religious wedding because of their perceptions about when such weddings were available or how they operated in practice.

Consistent with the general perception of the limited nature of the legal options, some did not think that getting married in a religious wedding was a possibility for them. This was the case for both Manizeh and Jane. As the latter mused:

'I would have preferred to just have one ceremony. The one that I wanted. ... And you know, I've got friends in Ireland and friends in Scotland, and the Bahá'í ceremony is legal in both of those places, and it's just so much easier ... it's such a shame for anybody that is ... unless you're Christian or Jewish ... your ceremony isn't legal, and it's just like there's so many people of so many faiths that just would want to do what they want to do that aren't recognized.'[32]

As a same-sex couple, Emma and Ellis may well also have assumed that their options for a religious wedding would have been limited; however, in this case even the 'believing' party, Ellis, evinced no desire for a religious wedding, noting that "even when I was a very practising Christian, I never thought about getting married in a church".

Others were aware of the option of getting married in a registered place of worship but disliked the way in which the legal elements intruded into such weddings and had therefore opted for a separate civil wedding. Interestingly, the resolutely atheist Jay was even more critical than his Jain wife, Jasmine, about the disruption occasioned by the presence of the registrar:

Jay:	It ruins the actual ceremony because they stop ... all the Indian stuff stops and then you've got this registrar turn up and he has to go through the legal stuff and it sort of ruins the ...
Jasmine:	The flow of it.
Jay:	... the theatre of what you're trying to create. And obviously the whole point of an Indian wedding is the theatre, the magic, the going back to this tradition, and it's all an auspicious occasion.

Respecting beliefs: choosing a religious ceremony

What came across very strongly in the interviews was that the person without religious beliefs recognized the importance of their partner's beliefs.[33] In every such case in our sample, if one partner had wanted a religious ceremony, the

---

[32] Seven Bahá'í centres – those in Brighton and Hove, Burnley, Fallowfield, Liverpool, London (Knightsbridge), Newcastle upon Tyne, and Whitfield – are registered for weddings: UK Government, 'Places of worship registered for marriage' (15 March 2015): www.gov.uk/government/publications/places-of-worship-registered-for-marriage

[33] This point was made by Manizeh: "He always knew that the religious part was important to me"; Rhoda: "He's very supportive of my beliefs and I support him on his beliefs";

other was willing to accede to it.[34] This again might be seen as unsurprising given the nature of our sample: since inclusion in our study depended on a couple having had a non-legally binding ceremony, it by definition did not include those who *only* had a civil wedding. Nonetheless, it was significant that so many of these unshared-faith couples did opt for a specifically religious ceremony rather than, for example, one led by a Humanist or independent celebrant that included elements of religion; just two couples chose the latter option.[35]

Only a few interviewees specifically mentioned how their partner had navigated the expressions of belief required as part of their ceremony. Phoebe, who had rejected the idea of a religious wedding, had been lucky to find a Methodist minister who was happy to conduct a blessing at her woodland wedding:

'He was just soon on board. And so enthusiastic and willing to accommodate what we wanted and to help ... really help us celebrate what we wanted to do and how we wanted to be ... I suppose how we wanted to be joined together. And that made [my husband] a lot more comfortable, to know that he understood and he was happy with that.'

Others reported that the religious dimension of the ceremony had not been an issue for their spouse. Jane noted that her husband "didn't mind saying the vow which mentions God", adding "we had spoken about it before, that it could mean whatever he wants it to mean. God can mean ... the universe". Rhoda even shared that her husband had taken Communion with her during their Church of England blessing. While this had not been his usual practice when attending services with her, she explained that:

'on the day, he partook in the Communion we had as just the two of us, because he was like, "well, it's the two of us doing it together", and he was pretty easy-going with everything. He was like, whatever we want. Because he was raised in a Church of England school so he was used to this kind of stuff being there ... singing hymns or hearing

---

Meera: "He ... respects the religion"; and Ellis: "Emma ... does have a very good understanding of Christianity and religion and a good respect for it as well."

[34] Manizeh said, "there was no ... there wasn't even a discussion. It was almost like this is how we're going to do it". Jane commented, "he was just really like, 'Yeah, we'll do whatever you want to do'". Rhoda said, "he's like, 'you want to go and have a blessing? We will have a blessing'". Meera commented, "he was just like, 'whatever you want to do, I'm quite happy to do it'".

[35] Karen and Sita both had an additional ceremony led by an independent celebrant: see further Chapter 8.

a Bible verse every now and then, or stuff like that. He didn't feel uncomfortable with any of it. He was like, "just because I'm doing this doesn't change how I believe, but it doesn't make me feel like I'm a bad person for doing it or anything like that".'

As this illustrates, unshared beliefs could be moderated by the couple's shared religious background and cultural expectations about the form that a wedding should take. This was particularly evident in the case of Jasmine and Jay. While they spoke of making certain changes to the format of their Jain ceremony, these changes were intended to modernize the ceremony rather than to modify its religiosity. Despite his atheism, Jay made no objection to any of the religious rituals and throughout the interview was just as likely as Jasmine to refer to it as "our Indian wedding".

As for the different-faith couples, the beliefs of family members of unshared-faith couples played an important role in determining what ceremonies took place. The importance of familial expectations was articulated by Adnan, who described himself as "agnostic" but from a Muslim background and who had married a Catholic. His case was therefore similar to that of different-faith couples in that he felt an obligation to comply with two separate religious traditions. As he explained, his civil wedding had been followed by two non-legally binding religious ceremonies:

'It was a way of satisfying both of our families, simply because we wanted to get married of course, but in terms of the ceremonies themselves, my mum especially is really religious, and it was very important for her that if I were to be in a relationship, that would be in the form of a marriage and also that it would be a Muslim wedding. ... So, that was kind of where we started. That was ... I don't want to say a requirement, but it was something that I had always been very clear about in my own head ... that that would have potentially led to an estrangement with my mother if I didn't go down that route. ... And then, from there, it kind of only seemed fair to do the Catholic ceremony as well.'

Conclusion

As we have shown in this chapter, the choices and constraints that apply when couples do not share the same beliefs as each other are complex. To the extent that couples' choices are constrained by law, the implementation of the Law Commission's recommendations would remove many of the current barriers. There would no longer be legal provisions limiting Jewish weddings to couples where both profess the Jewish religion, and the rules that limit couples to marrying in a limited range of registered places of worship would disappear. The Law Commission also envisages that organizations such as the OneSpirit Interfaith Foundation would qualify as belief organizations and be able to nominate officiants.

Whether increasing the range of options would lead to more legal weddings that include elements of different beliefs will depend on couples' own preferences. How couples with different beliefs reach their decision as to the form of their wedding is likely to remain complex, but at the very least, the sense of inequality that was so apparent in the interviews should disappear.

6

Paganism and the Desire to Be
Married Outdoors

'Getting married inside isn't the same for us. It has to be outside.'[1]

Introduction

So far, our focus has primarily been on the ways in which couples navigate the current legal framework. In this chapter and Chapters 7, 8, and 9, we consider the types of ceremonies for which the law in England and Wales makes no provision at present. We begin in this chapter with outdoor Pagan ceremonies.

In some respects, the issues facing Pagan couples are the same as those facing any other religious group with few buildings registered for weddings. At least since the decision of the Supreme Court in *Hodgkin*,[2] there is no issue with Pagan places of worship being certified as such and registered for weddings. However, for many Pagans, their sacred space is not a building at all, so the option of being married in a registered place of worship does not cohere with their beliefs. In addition, the ceremonies of Pagans in our sample were very different from those of other religious groups in terms of their format and who conducted them, and interviewees were noticeably less certain as to whether their beliefs would (or should) be recognized as 'religious'. For these reasons, we think that Pagan ceremonies merit separate consideration.

In this chapter, we begin by examining the plurality of Pagan beliefs and the (limited) options for Pagan weddings within the current legal framework. We then provide a description of a Pagan ceremony and identify the elements that mean the current legal framework generally does not work for Pagan

---

[1]   Murron, a Druid priestess.
[2]   *R (Hodkin) v Registrar General of Births, Deaths and Marriages* [2013] UKSC 77.

couples, before concluding by considering how the Law Commission's recommendations would work for them.

Pagan beliefs

'Paganism' is essentially an umbrella term for a range of different beliefs or paths.[3] When completing the 2021 Census, around 95,000 individuals identified their religion as 'Pagan', 'Wicca' or 'Shamanism'.[4] As Finn commented:

> 'You can go Animism, Shamanism, now you've American Shamanism, Celtic Shamanism. You're going to have North tradition. You can have an Anglo-Saxon tradition. You can have more Viking, more towards the Norse. You can head up and do Orkney-type stuff. You can have Wiccan. You can have ... Alexandrian, Gardnerian, you have various forms of Druidry. It's a broad family.'

The plurality of Paganism was reflected in the way that the Pagan study participants defined their beliefs and affiliations. For example, May and Murron both initially described themselves as Pagan but then specified that they were Druid; moreover, each belonged to different orders of Druids – unsurprising given Finn's comment that "there's probably somewhere in the region of about at least a dozen different orders of Druids in Britain". Finn himself explained that he had been involved with a Druid order and Shamanism but would now describe himself as Animistic if he was "going to apply any badge to it". And Stella, an interfaith minister within the OneSpirit Interfaith Foundation, was similarly averse to putting a label on her beliefs:

> 'I don't know, every time I have to fill in a form about what religion I am, I hesitate and think what am I going to put today? Because I hate putting myself in a box, cos it never feels like it does it justice, and yet it feels really important to me that I say I am something. So,

---

[3]   For discussion of the plurality within Paganism, see Graham Harvey (2016) 'Paganism' in Linda Woodhead, Christopher Partridge, and Hiroko Kawanami (eds) *Religions in the Modern World: Traditions and Transformations* (Routledge, 3rd ed). On the term itself, see Christopher P. Jones (2012) 'The fuzziness of "Paganism"' 18 *Common Knowledge* 249.

[4]   Office for National Statistics (2022) 'Religion, England and Wales: Census 2021' (29 November). This number may be an underestimate, as some Pagans may not wish to identify themselves as such on an official form: see Vivienne Crowley (2014) 'Standing up to be counted: understanding Pagan responses to the 2011 British censuses' 44 *Religion* 483, Table 1.

[one of the] other phrases that I've experimented with is "holistic". Yeah, so "earth-based", "holistic", "Pagan", but none of them quite fit.'

All interviewees who identified as Pagan described their beliefs as playing an important role in their lives. It was correspondingly important to them that their spouse shared those beliefs: thus, May explained that although her spouse, Hazel, was not in the same Druid order, she was still a Pagan "and we do … yeah, we have very, very similar outlooks and practices", while Amber, Grainne, and Murron all explained how their respective husbands had moved from understanding to sharing their beliefs. As Murron commented, "it makes a massive difference … in a relationship".

However, across our sample as a whole, Pagan participants were the most likely to speak of experiencing a lack of understanding of their religion, discrimination, and even overt hostility. Grainne was uncertain as to whether Druidry would be classified as a religion, commenting "it's classified as a religion now. But it doesn't really … nobody really says much about that. Legally it doesn't".[5] Dawn explained how she "almost felt a bit discriminated against" as a Pagan. And Murron referred to hostile commentary on social media from what she described as "Gospel awareness groups", and to having to be careful when describing Paganism to others. As she noted: "It doesn't always go down well with people, unfortunately. It's a shame because it's such a lovely nature-loving religion."

The options for Pagan weddings

As Gwydion, who conducted Pagan weddings, commented in relation to the conditions for buildings to be registered as places of worship, "we simply do not have those buildings". Among our interviewees, Murron had looked into the possibility of having a legally binding handfasting in the one building that is registered, the Goddess Temple at Glastonbury. Her decision not to marry there – on account of the logistical challenge of getting friends and family, together with members of the Order, to this particular venue – illustrates how having the legal option to marry in a particular place is not the same as having a realistic option of doing so.

For those without easy access to Glastonbury, there may still be the option of having a Pagan wedding in a registered place of worship of

---

5   For analysis of the somewhat chequered relationship between Paganism and the legal system of England and Wales, see G.F. Wheeler (2017) 'Witches, Odin and the English state: the legal reception of a counter-cultural minority religious movement' 32 *Journal of Law and Religion* 449.

another denomination. Gwydion floated the possibility of conducting a Pagan wedding in "an appropriate friendly Unitarian church", although he explained that this was more common in the United States and added, "I don't have any friendly Unitarians locally and I've never been asked to do that". He had, however, conducted one wedding in a Buddhist temple "for a Pagan–Buddhist wedding with a Buddhist bride".

In the absence of registered places of worship, the recent moves to make it easier to marry outdoors will not necessarily make it any easier for Pagans to marry in the form of their choosing. Since 1 July 2021, it has been possible for civil weddings to take place in an outdoor area that is linked to approved premises.[6] This option might well have been welcomed by Murron had it been available when she married, as her legal wedding took place at a hotel that was approved for weddings and her Pagan ceremony was in the hotel grounds later that same day.[7] However, being able to have her legal wedding outdoors would not have addressed the fact that she wanted her handfasting to be the ceremony that counted. As she emphasized, the legal wedding had taken place "very discreetly" a couple of hours before the majority of their guests had arrived, because they had wanted everyone to see the handfasting as their marriage.

Pagan ceremonies

A Pagan ceremony

Given the plurality within Paganism, it is unsurprising that there is no prescribed form for a Pagan wedding.[8] Instead, as Finn and Gwydion both emphasized, Pagan priests and priestesses work with couples to design ceremonies tailored to them.

To illustrate the kind of elements that a Pagan ceremony might include, we draw on the detailed account given by Grainne. As she explained, she had spent a long time searching for a religion that resonated with her, eventually finding it in a form of Druidism that shared similarities with Animism:

---

[6] This option was initially made available on a temporary basis and subsequently made permanent by the Marriage and Civil Partnerships (Approved Premises) (Amendment) Regulations 2022, SI 2022, No 295.

[7] Among our other interviewees, Hazel and May had considered getting married at a hotel that was approved for weddings, but noted that it was "phenomenally expensive" and "just wasn't right for us". Amber had her legal wedding on approved premises a year and a day after her first ceremony; she, however, was happy for that to be purely civil, explaining, "I didn't want a religious ceremony in that circumstance, because we'd already done that".

[8] For a selection of rituals, see Raven Kaldera and Tannin Schwartzstein (2011) *Inviting Hera's Blessing: Handfasting and Wedding Rituals* (Llewellyn Publications).

'My background is that I'm a scientist by training, so I tend to … for years I've wanted some sort of … something I can touch and feel rather than a god in the sky. But, having said that, as I've got older, my beliefs now are that everything has spirit. The rocks, the trees, the earth … we owe a lot to the earth. We all live as one. So, earth, sky, moon, sun, seas, air, sea, sky, earth … all that resonates with me now. Living in harmony with nature.'

Those beliefs had been central to her Pagan ceremony, which had taken place a few days after her register office wedding. To ensure that the ceremony was led by people who shared her beliefs, she had asked two friends to do it:

'It was important for me to have somebody doing the ceremony that I knew and that knew what we were doing, who had the same beliefs as me. Because I didn't want a celebrant or somebody to do it if they don't have that belief, because anybody can go in and call up the spirits and read the writing, but if they're not doing it properly, to me it makes no sense. It's not hypocritical, but it just doesn't make sense.'

While the friends in question had "never done anything like that before", Grainne reported that they were "thrilled" to be asked.

The ceremony itself took place at a historic site on top of a hill that she described as her "temple in nature". She went on to say:

'And it's a very high but quite special place … it's just a beautiful place to be and, for me, the elements are all there. You feel like you're in the air when you're on there. And all the water around you … the rivers … and you've got the earth. So, that's the place we chose.'

At the site, she had arranged to have an altar, "which was a piece of holly wood cut down the centre". On this, they had placed hawthorn flowers, a candle, and a dish with water from the local river. As both she and her husband had lost their fathers, "their pictures were on the altar to honour them".

The friends officiating at the ceremony took the guests up to the top of the hill, where they formed a circle. Grainne and her husband then walked up the hill to join them and the ceremony began:

'So, we started by consecrating the circle and opening up the circle to the spirits of the north, south, east, and west. Calling to air, sea, and sky. And calling in those spirits to be with us in that ceremony. And the call for peace as well. And we called to the ancestors. So, the ancestors of the land where we are … people that have gone before us. The birds ... the wildlife, all that sort of thing. And then the circle is open and we concentrated on the marriage ceremony itself. So, we are brought in and stand with each other and we are asked questions and say our vows, which we had written ourselves about how we felt.'

Just as they were saying their vows, she looked up and a kestrel was hovering in the air in front of them:

'And I could hear everybody going [intake of breath] ... nobody spoke as this thing just hovered in front of us and then it was off. And ... sometimes little things like that and you think, wow. You sort of shiver because you can't describe how you feel at that particular time when something like that joins you.'

They had then asked for blessings from the north, south, east, and west, each symbolizing a different element and emotion (for example, north representing the earth and stability). As they went round each of the quarters, different family members stepped forward to participate in the blessing.

'And then, once we had our blessings, then we had our handfasting cord, which I had woven and made. And that's tied around the hands to bind you together in your love. ... So, we did that and then we had some mead and some ... apple cake. So, we drink mead from the mead horn ... I offer that to my partner and he offers it to me. We drink from the mead horn. We give a little bit to earth first before we do that, and to the spirits. And then we go around the circle and everybody drinks from the mead horn. And then I do the same with the cake. He feeds me, I feed him, a little bit for earth, and then we go around again and everybody had a little bit of apple cake. And then when we finish the ceremony ... in a similar way we close down the four quarters, we thank the spirits for being with us and then when we finished, ... everybody made an archway and we ran through and back. And we also jumped ... in Paganism you can jump the broom. It signifies going from one life into the next ... one phase of your life into the next. Well, we did it with poles, with staffs. So, we crossed those and we stepped over those symbolically ... it was just absolutely magical.'

Key elements of Pagan ceremonies

While Grainne's ceremony was unique, there were certain key elements that recurred in the accounts given by other Pagan participants: the importance of particular sacred spaces; the range of rituals on which they drew; and the importance of knowing the person who was to conduct the ceremony. Another key aspect is the level of commitment that the parties make.

Sacred spaces

In explaining the importance of being able to have a wedding outdoors, participants highlighted the religious or spiritual significance attached to nature within different strands of Paganism: Murron, for example, noted that "Druids practise out in nature", and Amber described Wicca as "very nature-based in its connection". More generally, May thought that being able to be married outdoors "would be enormously beneficial to the Pagan community" as a whole, noting: "Unless you are invested in religious buildings, like churches and things, I don't really see why it should be indoors. Especially for nature religion. It's just not desirable to be indoors for it."

Scholars have also identified the significance attached by Pagans to specific 'sacred' sites.[9] Amber and Gaia both described ceremonies taking place at sites such as Stonehenge or other stone circles. Others, like Grainne, identified their sense of connection to a particular part of the landscape: Hazel and May described how they had identified a place on the moor that was 'sacred' to them, with May explaining that it had "a lovely hawthorn tree and a natural, big slab, which makes a natural altar".

A plurality of rituals

The ceremonies described by May and Murron contained many of the same elements as Grainne's: both had included a ritual welcoming of the four elements, handfasting, and jumping over a broomstick; Murron and her husband had shared mead; and Hazel and May had shared some baklava, although May described this as "probably taken possibly from more Jewish tradition when you put the sweets in each other's mouths and say 'may our shared words always be sweet'". Hazel and May had also made an offering to the Hindu god Ganesha (as well as other gods, ancestors, and absent friends). As this indicates, individuals saw themselves as drawing on a rich range of ideas and practices in constructing a ceremony that was right for them.[10]

When asked if there was a specific point in the ceremony at which the couple would be regarded as married, Gwydion said there was a point when he would declare the couple to be married, while Finn noted that it would depend on what the couple saw as the "defining moment" spiritually.

---

[9]   See, for example, Jenny Blain and Robert J. Wallis (2004) 'Sacred sites, contested rites/
      rights: contemporary Pagan engagements with the past' 9 *Journal of Material Culture* 237.
[10] For discussion of the eclecticism of Pagan source material, see Harvey (2016).

Knowing the person who is leading the ceremony

It was striking that *all* of the ceremonies reported by interviewees with Pagan beliefs had been conducted by a friend or friends.[11] In the case of Stella, this friend was also an interfaith minister, but in the cases of Amber, Hazel, and May, the friends had no prior experience of conducting ceremonies.[12] For May, this was part of an anticlerical stance: as she explained, "I didn't want someone to come and be like the official intercessor to the divine".

Finn similarly commented that couples wanted "people of the same spirituality ... who can bring that sacredness that they want within that commitment to each other"; he explained that he only conducted ceremonies when "people that know me and know that I do it ... come to me and ask". Gwydion commented that when finding a celebrant for a Pagan ceremony had depended on word of mouth, it used to be "friends and close associates" only, but the internet had enabled couples to find suitable celebrants more easily.

Different levels of commitment

While most participants who identified as Pagan referred to handfasting in terms of the specific ritual of hands being bound together, Finn explained that a handfasting had three possible levels: for a year and a day, for this lifetime, or for all lifetimes to come. Amber was the only participant who had initially chosen a handfasting for a year and a day, as a means of testing the relationship before making a binding legal commitment. She explained that "it's like a test run to see if it works, because from my own personal perspective, people can change when they get married. There's this feminist fight-or-flight-type thing for me, where it was like I need to know that there's not this bind and that it can work and he's not going to change". For Amber, as a survivor of domestic abuse, this wish to test the relationship had particular significance. It should, however, be noted that the law does not recognize time-limited marriages and there are no proposals for this to change. As a result, couples looking to have a handfasting predetermined to last a year and a day will only be able to do so via a non-legally binding ceremony, as otherwise they would need to seek a divorce to end their marriage.

---

[11] Although in the case of Amber, this was pure happenstance; as she explained, "we were supposed to have a priestess that was going to come and perform the ceremony, but she backed out at the last minute. Or just didn't turn up, which was very disappointing, but our friend instead did the ceremony for us".

[12] Murron also noted that she had asked two friends from her Order to perform the ceremony, but did not mention whether they had conducted ceremonies for others.

Conclusion

As the Law Commission noted in its report on weddings reform, it is clear that the law's concept of religion already encompasses Pagan religions.[13] Under the Law Commission's scheme, the ability of Pagan groups to conduct legal weddings would no longer depend on whether they worship in a building, but rather on whether they meet the criteria for nominating officiants.

Reflecting on the characteristics of the Pagan ceremonies described within our study, the Law Commission's recommendations relating to the location and the content of the ceremony would have clear benefits for couples wishing to have a legally recognized Pagan wedding. It would be possible for a ceremony to take place not just outside a building, but in the kinds of locations described by Amber, Grainne, Hazel, and May. Moreover, with the removal of prescribed words, the binding of hands – or such other ceremonial moment agreed by the parties and the officiant – could constitute the moment at which the parties are legally married. On the publication of the report, one Pagan priest commented '[f]or pagan couples to be able to have the ceremony of their faith and it be legal would be amazing after all these years'.[14]

The main issue for Pagan couples would be the need for an authorized officiant. But as we have noted, the officiant does not need to conduct the ceremony. The possibility of splitting the roles of officiant and celebrant would mean that couples would be able to have the ceremony conducted by the person of their choosing, even if they were not authorized, as long as an officiant was present to ensure that the legal requirements were met. While this would be more expensive than asking a friend to lead the ceremony, it would avoid the necessity of having a separate civil wedding.

---

[13] Law Commission (2022) *Celebrating Marriage: A New Weddings Law* (19 July), para 4.137.

[14] Connie Dimsdale (2022) 'With this handfasting, I thee wed', *i weekend*, 23 July.

7

Belief in Humanist Ceremonies

'The point about Humanist ceremonies is Humanism is a recognized belief system. ... If people are Humanist, they should be able to have a legal Humanist ceremony like a legal Catholic ceremony or Church of England ceremony.'[1]

Introduction

Weddings law in England and Wales – in contrast to the position in Scotland, Northern Ireland, and the Republic of Ireland[2] – currently makes no provision for non-religious belief organizations to conduct weddings. In recent years, this lack of provision has attracted increasing attention and criticism.[3] It has also been the subject of judicial review in *R (ota Harrison) v Secretary of State for Justice*.[4] In that case, Eady J took the view that having a Humanist wedding would amount to a manifestation of Humanist beliefs for the purposes of Article 9 of the European Convention on Human

---

[1] Joyce, Humanist celebrant.
[2] On which see, respectively, Murray McLean (2018) 'Beyond belief: the law and practice of marriage formation in contemporary Scotland' 30 *Child and Family Law Quarterly* 237; Sharon Thompson and Frank Cranmer (2019) 'Humanist weddings in Northern Ireland: a missed opportunity for reform?' 41 *Journal of Social Welfare and Family Law* 229; Susan Leahy and Kathryn O'Sullivan (2018) 'Changing conceptions of marriage in Ireland: law and practice' 20 *Child and Family Law Quarterly* 279.
[3] For discussion, see All-Party Parliamentary Humanist Group (2018) *'Any Lawful Impediment?'; A report of the All-Party Parliamentary Humanist Group's inquiry into the legal recognition of humanist marriage in England and Wales* (All-Party Parliamentary Humanist Group).
[4] *R (ota Harrison) v Secretary of State for Justice* [2020] EWHC 2096 (Admin).

Rights.[5] She also found that the claimants – six Humanist couples – were in an analogous position to persons holding religious beliefs who wished to manifest that belief when getting married, but were treated differently from such couples. As she concluded, 'subject *only* to the question of justification – the present law gives rise to article 14 discrimination in the Claimants' enjoyment of their article 9 rights'.[6]

Our aim in this chapter is not to chart the various attempts to make provision for Humanist weddings[7] or to explore the range of reasons why couples might opt for a Humanist ceremony.[8] Rather, as in previous chapters, our focus is on the limitations of the law in allowing for couples to marry in accordance with their beliefs.[9] We first show how these limitations are not intrinsic to the framework established by the Marriage Act 1836 or its successor, but are in fact the result of late 20th-century judicial interpretation. We then go on to discuss how personalization is key to a Humanist ceremony, drawing on a case study from our project. We also explore the relationship between Humanist beliefs and the choice of a Humanist ceremony, as discussed by participants in our study, and the extent to which a Humanist ceremony may also include reference to religious beliefs.

Accommodating non-religious beliefs

As discussed in Chapter 3, the legal framework established by the Marriage Act 1836 was designed to ensure that no one should be required to marry in a way that was incompatible with their conscience. This was reflected in the absence of any requirement that a ceremony in a registered place of worship be conducted in accordance with religious rites. The evidence suggests that this absence was a deliberate policy decision, influenced by a high-profile example of a non-legally binding ceremony taking place in a

---

[5]   *R (ota Harrison) v Secretary of State for Justice* [2020], [68]. As Eady J noted, however, for the purposes of their claim, the claimants only had to show that the conduct of a Humanist marriage fell within the ambit of Article 9.

[6]   *R (ota Harrison) v Secretary of State for Justice* [2020], [124]. Having considered the issue of justification, she refused to make a declaration of incompatibility, on the basis that the Secretary of State had 'demonstrated a legitimate aim in seeking to address this issue as part of a wider reform': [117].

[7]   On which see Russell Sandberg (2021) *Religion and Marriage Law: The Need for Reform* (Bristol University Press), ch 5.

[8]   On which see Rebecca Probert, Rajnaara C. Akhtar, and Sharon Blake (2022) *When Is a Wedding Not a Marriage? Exploring non-legally binding ceremonies: Final Report* (Nuffield Foundation), 97–101.

[9]   Our focus is therefore on those ceremonies that were specifically conducted by celebrants accredited by Humanists UK rather than on ceremonies that our individuals described as Humanist in the sense of being non-religious.

chapel with no reference to any deity or religious beliefs.[10] In other words, couples who held non-religious beliefs were not limited to marrying in a register office, but could also do so in a registered place of worship.

Moreover, exactly what constituted a 'place of religious worship' was surprisingly flexible in the early years of the Act's operation. In 1840, the Hall of Science in Sheffield was registered for weddings.[11] The Hall of Science was one of the meeting places of the Owenites,[12] a utopian socialist movement that sought to create a 'New Moral World'. Its central body was the Universal Community Society of Rational Religionists, and it adopted many of the forms of a religion while rejecting belief in a deity.[13] However, the registration, like the movement itself, proved to be relatively short-lived.

Of somewhat longer duration was the registration of the meeting places of various Ethical Societies. The best-known is the South Place Ethical Society, a group that had its origins in a religious organization and whose original premises had been one of the first places of worship to be registered for weddings under the 1836 Act. Its premises remained registered for weddings after it moved away from its religious roots. But the South Place Ethical Society was just one of a number of similar societies that combined in 1896 to form the Union of Ethical Societies.[14] One ethical society's meeting place, Mall Hall, was 'duly certified for religious worship' and registered for weddings in 1909, to be replaced a year later by the Ethical Church in Bayswater, led by the American Stanton Coit.[15]

Stanton had himself had an additional 'ethical ceremonial' after his register office wedding in 1898.[16] At the ceremony, Frederic Harrison, another key figure within the movement, delivered a speech in which he explained that the group 'met to welcome as husband and wife those who in an ampler form desired to renew the vows of wedlock, which they had just made

[10] For discussion of this case, see Rebecca Probert (2021) *Tying the Knot: The Formation of Marriage 1836–2020* (Cambridge University Press), and (2022) 'Secular or sacred? The ambiguity of "civil" marriage in the Marriage Act 1836' 43 *Journal of Legal History* 136.

[11] *London Gazette* (1840) 3 April.

[12] John Salt (1960) 'The Sheffield Hall of Science' 12 *The Vocational Aspect of Secondary and Further Education* 133.

[13] J.F.C. Harrison (1969) *Robert Owen and the Owenites in Britain and America: The Quest for the New Moral World* (Routledge & Kegan Paul); Eileen Yeo (1971) 'Robert Owen and radical culture' in Sidney Pollard and John Salt (eds) *Robert Owen: Prophet of the Poor* (Macmillan).

[14] Colin Campbell (1971) *Towards a Sociology of Irreligion* (Macmillan).

[15] *London Gazette* (1909) 19 October, 7687, and (1910) 14 January. Another Ethical Church was registered for weddings in Toxteth: *London Gazette* (1915) 3 December.

[16] *Reynolds' Newspaper* (1898) 'Marriage of Dr. Stanton Coit: An ethical ceremonial' 25 December. This additional ceremony took place in Kensington Town Hall, a few minutes' walk away from the register office in Cheniston Lodge on Marloes Road.

before the representative of the law'; Harrison then invited Stanton and his wife to 'stand in the face of the congregation and recite the words which custom had sanctioned, and which the Church adopted from the ancients, to be used as the symbols of marriage'.[17]

The fact that these were isolated examples in part reflects the relative lack of enthusiasm for what Clive Field has termed 'organized irreligion' at this time.[18] In his account of the waning social significance of religion from the 19th century to the end of the Second World War, he noted that membership of secularist organizations was relatively small and even fell during the inter-war period. In the light of the fact that he identified the South Place Ethical Society as the largest of the ethical societies, it is worth noting that it appears that the number of weddings celebrated by it at Conway Hall was very small.

Humanism in its modern sense emerged in the mid-20th century. The British Humanist Association was initially formed in 1963 'as a "common front organization" for the Ethical Union and the Rationalist Press Association',[19] but the latter organization removed its support when the former lost its charitable status on account of its political objectives. In 1967, the British Humanist Association resolved to amend its articles of association to enable it to campaign as a political pressure group.[20]

At that time, its campaigns did not include changes to the laws governing weddings, perhaps because Humanists still had the option of being married at Conway Hall. The following decade, however, the flexibility that had enabled it to be registered for weddings came to an end following the decision of the Court of Appeal in *R v Registrar General, ex parte Segerdal*. That case had held that a building could only be certified as a place of worship – the prerequisite for being registered for weddings – if its principal use was 'as a place where people come together as a congregation or assembly to do reverence to God'.[21] While that particular case had involved the Church of Scientology, the reasoning was equally applicable to the South Place Ethical

---

[17] *Reynolds' Newspaper* (1898), 5. The following year, Stanton himself was reported as acting as the 'celebrant' for what one newspaper described as 'a marriage ceremony carried out in accordance with the rites, if such a term may be used, of the Ethical Society': *Lloyd's* (1899) 'An Ethical wedding at Battersea' 27 August; *Bristol Mercury* (1899) 'Unique matrimonial ceremony' 29 August. Again, the legal wedding had taken place previously at the register office.

[18] Clive Field (2019) *Periodizing Secularization: Religious Allegiance and Attendance in Britain, 1880–1945* (Oxford University Press).

[19] Colin Campbell (1969) 'Humanism in Britain: the formation of a secular value-oriented movement' in David Martin (ed) *A Sociological Yearbook of Religion in Britain 2* (SCM Press Ltd), 160.

[20] *The Times* (1967) 'Humanists join the political fray: shedding charitable status' 14 January.

[21] *R v Registrar General, ex parte Segerdal* [1970] 2 QB 697, at 707.

Society, and in 1977 its registration for weddings was cancelled. Subsequent litigation over its charitable purposes resulted in the High Court drawing a clear line between religion and ethics. As the judge noted:

> It is natural that the court should desire not to discriminate between beliefs deeply and sincerely held, whether they are beliefs in a god or in the excellence of man or in ethical principles or in Platonism or some other scheme of philosophy. But I do not see that that warrants extending the meaning of the word 'religion' so as to embrace all other beliefs and philosophies. Religion, as I see it, is concerned with man's relations with God, and ethics are concerned with man's relations with man. The two are not the same, and are not made the same by sincere inquiry into the question: what is God? If reason leads people not to accept Christianity or any known religion, but they do believe in the excellence of qualities such as truth, beauty and love, or believe in the platonic concept of the ideal, their beliefs may be to them the equivalent of a religion, but viewed objectively they are not religion.[22]

Since then, the options available to the growing number of Humanist couples[23] have been more limited. While there is nothing in the terms of the Marriage Act 1949 to prevent a place of worship from *hosting* a Humanist ceremony, whether that is an option in practice will depend on the permission of its governing authority. One guide to Humanist weddings noted that there were examples of Humanist weddings taking place in Unitarian churches 'either with the minister conducting a non-religious wedding, or merely registering the marriage after allowing a Humanist to conduct the actual ceremony'.[24] Similarly, there is nothing in the terms of the Marriage Act 1949 to prevent a civil wedding from including Humanist content or even from being led by a Humanist celebrant.[25] However, as Eady J pointed out in *Harrison*, a Humanist ceremony 'will not, of itself, be

---

[22] *In re South Place Ethical Society* [1980] 1 WLR 1565, at 1571.

[23] It was noted in *Harrison* that Humanists UK had around 85,000 members and supporters and that 6 per cent of the population had identified themselves as non-religious and Humanist in a 2018 YouGov poll.

[24] Jane Wynne Willson (1996) *Sharing the Future: A Practical Guide to Non-religious Wedding Ceremonies* (British Humanist Association), 4.

[25] There was some dispute on this point in *Harrison*, but the position of the Secretary of State, supported by the General Register Office, was that 'there need be only one ceremony, which can incorporate humanist elements and can be conducted by a humanist celebrant, provided that this is in the presence of a superintendent registrar and registrar', a position which Eady J thought was 'entirely consistent with the requirements of the 1949 Act': *R (ota Harrison) v Secretary of State for Justice* [2020], [80].

given legal recognition absent the presence of officials who need have no connection with humanism'.[26] Alternatively, where the civil wedding takes place on approved premises, it may be accompanied by a separate Humanist ceremony. Within our study, however, a number of Humanist celebrants spoke of venues being under pressure not to allow this.

In addition, as a number of Humanist celebrants emphasized, the personalization involved in Humanist weddings meant that it was also important for the ceremony to be conducted in a place that held significance for the couple.

A Humanist ceremony

As noted in *Harrison*, the 'Usages for humanist marriages' published by Humanists UK stipulate that the ceremony 'must include a preamble from a trained and accredited Humanists UK celebrant that gives a brief but explicit description of humanist beliefs'.[27] Among our participants, Faye explained her celebrant "wrote some of the ceremony talking about the way that Humanists marry people".

Apart from such framing, it is of the essence of Humanist weddings that they are personalized. As one Humanist celebrant, Joyce, explained, "there is no set Humanist wedding. It's always about the couple". Another, Margaret, expanded on this to explain how the content of the ceremony would be devised:

'Humanist ceremonies are about celebrating life and the couple, sharing the couples' story, their dreams and aspirations. They are written based on what values are most important to that couple. There's freedom of choice, which is not available in a civil ceremony, like the venue, the celebrant, the order and the length of the ceremony, the symbolic actions, and it's a ceremony that is written collaboratively. So, the couple have full input, full control over edits, which again is not available in a civil ceremony.'

In order to give a sense of what a Humanist wedding ceremony might look like, in this section we draw on Helen's account of her ceremony. Helen, like her husband, was an atheist and a Humanist, and those beliefs shaped her day-to-day living and decision-making. They had found a local Humanist celebrant through Humanists UK's website; as Helen explained, "she came to meet us beforehand and, you know, we had a long chat about,

---

[26] *R (ota Harrison) v Secretary of State for Justice* [2020], [92].

[27] *R (ota Harrison) v Secretary of State for Justice* [2020], [28].

you know, what was important to us and who we were, and then she kind of developed the ceremony based on that".

The legal wedding took place in a register office on a Wednesday morning, with two friends as witnesses. It was, as Helen described, "the bare minimum". Lasting around 15 minutes, there were no readings, no music, and no exchange of rings, reflecting Helen's view that this element was "purely to do the legalities". Despite describing the ceremony itself as "impersonal", Helen commented that "the registrar was lovely"; they had told her that they were having a further ceremony and she had "wished us the best for our ceremony and everything".

The main Humanist ceremony took place the following Saturday as part of a whole weekend of events with around 120 guests. Helen explained that she and her husband were "massive music fans" and had planned the weekend as a festival:

'It was a beautiful location with a lake, and we put a big marquee up and lots of bell tents, and there's a river running through it. And we had a whole weekend. It was a proper festival ... it was just having the opportunity to bring everybody into one place to have fun, to be able to make it a whole celebration rather than, like, "You go there and you do your formal bit, and you go there and you do this, and you go there ... and then you're gonna go and have a reception, and then you're gonna go there for your drinks". Just like, you know, I just wanted everybody to be in one place to celebrate at the same time.'

It was also important for that place to be one that they "connected with". Having the ceremony outside was important to them; as Helen added, "nature's a huge part of our lives as well, and we wanted to be as close to it as possible".

The ceremony itself took place next to the lake. Helen and her husband exchanged vows that they had written themselves; as she laughingly admitted, her husband had "absolutely knocked it out of the park" in writing his vows: "Much better than mine, but they were completely personal to us, and incredibly touching and memorable; they were beautiful. Yeah. So that was absolutely lovely. Lots of tears, not a dry eye in the house."

The couple had also decided to have a handfasting as an opportunity for Helen's daughter from her first marriage to be involved in the ceremony: "She was the one that presented us with the ... the knot that you tie your hands together with." Her brother had read an excerpt from Philip Pullman, and a number of friends had spontaneously joined in singing a John Legend song.

When asked whether she would have preferred to have had a single combined ceremony that was legally recognized, her answer was clear:

'Definitely combine them. Yeah. Because there's no question that being legally recognized as married is important. It's important to me and my husband. But equally, if not more important, was the fact that we had a wedding that was personal, a ceremony that was personal to us, and reflected us as people individually and as a couple. So, to combine those two very important events to make that ceremony the ultimate important event absolutely would have been our choice.'

Reflecting non-religious beliefs

Research into Humanist weddings in other jurisdictions has demonstrated that the desire for a ceremony conducted by a Humanist celebrant extends beyond those who formally identify as Humanist.[28] That was reflected in our study too. Shelley was the only Humanist celebrant who specifically referred to conducting a ceremony for a couple who were "card-carrying Humanists" and "very firm in their convictions". None of the other Humanist celebrants mentioned whether the couples whose weddings they had conducted had held Humanist beliefs (although of course this may have been because to them, it was a given). Among those who had had (or had been considering) a Humanist wedding, only Helen actually defined herself as a Humanist.[29] By contrast, Linda explicitly stated that she did not "identify as a Humanist" but "probably atheist",[30] and when asked to describe "any religious or other beliefs", Alice replied simply "I don't have any".

For a couple of participants, the importance of being able to personalize the ceremony was that they did not have to make vows in which they did *not* believe. Faye commented that she would "feel like a complete hypocrite" if she married in a church, and Alice explained:

'The reason we went with a Humanist ceremony for the main day was both my husband and I … we don't have faith and so we knew that

---

[28] Murray McLean (2018) 'Beyond belief: the law and practice of marriage formation in contemporary Scotland' 30 *Child and Family Law Quarterly* 237; Agata Rejowska (2021) 'Humanist weddings in Poland: the various motivations of couples' 82 *Sociology of Religion* 281.

[29] In addition, Vicky initially defined herself as a "reluctant atheist" who would "like to believe that there is a god and an afterlife", but explained she and her partner had been considering a Humanist wedding as "we're probably closest to Humanists than anything else".

[30] As she explained, "I don't engage in my local Humanist group or anything like that". Humanist ceremonies were, however, an option with which she was already familiar, as her grandfather had been very active in the British Humanist Association and her aunt had had a Humanist ceremony.

we didn't want to get married in a church and be saying vows that we actually felt were contradicting our ways of life.'

She described the vows that she had exchanged with her husband as "nice, short, brief, honest ones". Shelley described those who did marry in a church despite their lack of belief as "slightly crossing your fingers or being a passive observer to some of those words, because you do not believe in them",[31] and she spoke passionately of the importance of being able to believe in the words spoken:

> 'When I got married in 2012 and I had a Humanist ceremony, I was actually more nervous than any kind of thousand gigs that I had ever done before. Because it was real; it was me. And it was me opening my ribcage and exposing my beating heart and saying truthful words and authentic words. ... Authenticity and truth matter on your wedding day. You've got to hear something you believe in and you've got to say something you believe in.'

Significantly, however, some interviewees who did not identify themselves as holding Humanist beliefs spoke of how they shared Humanist values. Faye had found out about Humanist ceremonies when looking into the possibility of getting married outside. As she explained:

> 'I found out about the Humanist celebrants and what they do, and the Humanist way of living, and I actually thought that's actually really like how I like to live my life anyway, with the Christian values I was brought up with but none of the actual religious stuff. That's what Humanism seems to me.'

As she had previously explained, her childhood had been heavily influenced by religion. Her grandfather had been a vicar, and she had been "brought up in a Protestant, C of E kind of way. Church, Sunday School, christenings, confirmations, the lot". After the death of her grandparents, her parents had asked her and her sister if they still wanted to go to church and they had decided that they did not. Nonetheless, she valued having had this type of upbringing:

---

[31] That sense of being a "passive observer" was very evident in the way that Helen spoke about her wedding to her first husband, which had taken place in a Catholic church. As she explained, the choice of wedding had been purely for the sake of her ex-husband and his family: "It didn't feel like it was anything to do with me, really. Which is a bit weird. So I suppose that kind of cemented in my mind how important it was to do something in a way that means something to you."

'to be able to say that you are kind of part of something, you know, you have ... not so much beliefs, but a certain way of living, of being, you know ... like a Christian way of living, I think, is a good way to go about things. You know, being a kind person, generous, you know, the Good Samaritan thing.'

Similarly, Simrat, who was brought up as a Sikh, felt that Humanist principles were something that she could share with her Hindu husband:

'I would say we're both very spiritual beings in the sense that I don't feel that I need to do anything religious necessarily. We are both individuals who just believe in the goodness of all and align on our Humanistic principles of just, you know, karma and just being a good human being. So, I don't really think that that's assigned to any religion per se. I think that that's the fundamentals of being a good human being. But there's crossovers in religion, so for me, I think it's quite a challenging concept. I would say my partner and I both align on our spiritual values. How that manifests more formally may differ, because I might actively think "oh, I might want to say a prayer", whereas I don't think that that's something he would like to do. So, I think spiritually we believe that there is a god and we align on that, but we don't ... we are not very formal in it.'

Reflecting religious beliefs in Humanist ceremonies

There was a strong perception among those who had chosen a Humanist ceremony that they would not have had the option of including any material with religious connotations in a civil wedding. Shelley commented that her Humanist ceremony had included some poetry by Andrew Motion that "had metaphorical spirituality references in them that were clearly metaphor and weren't at all religious" but which "wouldn't have been allowed in a civil ceremony". Alice reported that a friend who had married in a civil wedding "had asked for a particular reading and was told that they couldn't use it, because it had the word 'sheep' in it and sheep suggested shepherd and shepherd suggests Jesus". She also explained how her husband "didn't really like the idea of pandering to something that seemed so unreasonable in its prescriptiveness". She went on:

'The way he described it was that he pictured a load of old religious politicians a hundred years ago being so angry that there were people who wanted to get married outside of a religious set-up that they went, "well, fine, you can do it but you're not allowed to do it like this and you have to say it like this", because they were so indignant that there was any suggestion of doing anything other than a religious ceremony.'

While a Humanist ceremony is non-religious, some Humanist celebrants noted that it could be a neutral option for different-faith couples. As Andy noted: "You might have observing Muslims on one side of the room and hard-drinking cradle Catholics on the other side, but because it's not religious territory, they can both join in the wedding ceremony."

The willingness of Humanist celebrants to conduct ceremonies *for* couples who held religious beliefs did not mean that they were willing to conduct ceremonies *according to* religious beliefs. As Margaret noted, while they valued other faiths, "there is a difference between what we would include in terms of a religious line". Shelley explained that line in terms of the difference between culture and religion:

> 'We are in the main a secular society. The majority of people are non-religious in some way. But the difficulty in a post-religious society in this way is that culture and religion is still quite Velcroed together. And I often deal with the blurred lines between cultural significance and cultural qualities and gestures in a ceremony that matters with families throughout the ages. And actually what people believe. Because there are people who are culturally Jewish and they do want to have Jewish cultural gestures in their wedding ceremony, but that doesn't mean that they believe in God. It means that this is part of their heritage and this is part of their cultural observance and respect towards their families. But it doesn't mean that it's actually religious.'

The challenge of drawing these distinctions is particularly highlighted by the inclusion of handfasting in Humanist ceremonies. As mentioned, for Helen, handfasting was a ritual to involve her daughter in her Humanist ceremony, yet for the Pagan ceremonies described in the previous chapter, a handfasting is an important ritual within their religious ceremonies. Shelley suggested that "there is so much cultural heritage in society that means something sentimentally to people but actually isn't affixed to believing in a god or gods. And it should, and can be, recognized without it being an act of worship, which is what I do. And have done". Whether a ritual is perceived as reflecting beliefs, cultural traditions, or identity will depend on the individuals marrying, as we discuss further in the next chapter.

Conclusion

As Eady J concluded in *R (ota Harrison) v Secretary of State for Justice*:

For many humanists such ceremonies are not simply motivated or influenced by their beliefs; rather, there is an intimate link with the humanist belief system, in particular, in the way in which couples prepare for their wedding with their celebrant, in the statements made during the ceremony and in the emphasis on individual freedom of choice.[32]

When it came to the question of legal recognition, all four interviewees who had a Humanist ceremony were clear that they would have wanted that ceremony to be legally recognized, rather than having to have a separate legal wedding. As Helen explained, it was about having a single event that conferred legal recognition and reflected her and her spouse as a couple. Humanist celebrants also attached considerable importance to being able to conduct legal weddings. Joyce, who had conducted a legally binding ceremony in Scotland as a Humanists UK-accredited celebrant, reported that "it was absolutely magical to be able to do that, to have them signing that piece of paper, which actually represented the legality in that moment, was just incredible".

Humanist celebrants predicted that there would be more demand for the types of ceremony they conducted if couples did not have the hurdle of going through an additional ceremony in order to be legally married. Shelley noted that she was aware of couples opting for a single legal ceremony rather than having an additional Humanist ceremony on the grounds of cost and ease and "None of this question from your grandma about, 'is that the real wedding?'" She spoke passionately of how legal recognition would be "amazing", not least because it would convey that "essentially the government approves of us. Because, at the moment, it feels like the government are saying we're not real and we're not authentic and we're not needed".

As noted at the outset, the Law Commission was tasked with devising a scheme that could include ceremonies conducted by non-religious belief organizations. Under its scheme, a non-religious belief organization[33] will be able to nominate officiants on the same basis as a religious organization if the government choses to enable them to do so. That would enable the kinds of ceremonies discussed in this chapter to be conducted as legal weddings, bringing England and Wales into line with the rest of the United Kingdom and allowing Humanist couples to marry in accordance with their

---

[32] *R (ota Harrison) v Secretary of State for Justice* [2020], [69].

[33] A non-religious belief organization is defined as one 'whose sole or principal purpose is the advancement of a system of non-religious beliefs which have a level of cogency, seriousness, cohesion and importance that brings them within the meaning of Article 9 of the European Convention on Human Rights': Law Commission (2022) *Celebrating Marriage: A New Weddings Law* (19 July), para 4.257.

beliefs. As our study suggests that the values of authenticity and integrity are important in couples' choice of wedding whether or not the individuals subscribe to a formal system of beliefs, it is perhaps likely that the reach of Humanist celebrants will extend beyond those who hold Humanist beliefs, depending on what other options are available to couples. As Chapters 8 and 9 will show, there are other ways of accommodating those who do not align themselves with a formal system of beliefs.

8

Personalization and Beliefs: The Role of the Independent Celebrant

'Absolutely at the heart of what we do is a commitment. A heartfelt and a deeply felt commitment between these couples ... making vows that they intend to fulfil. Not saying words that they just have to repeat.'[1]

Introduction

In this chapter, we explore the relatively new phenomenon of ceremonies led by an independent celebrant. For present purposes, we define an independent celebrant as any person who conducts a range of different types of non-legally binding wedding ceremonies. They are independent of any religious, belief, or government organization and typically work as sole traders, although they will often be a member of a professional network that also provides accredited training.[2]

Ceremonies led by independent celebrants have proved increasingly popular in recent years. Stephanie Pywell's survey of independent celebrants concluded that it was likely that the number of celebrant-led ceremonies had more than doubled between 2015 and 2020, and estimated that there were between 9,000 and 10,000 such ceremonies taking place each year.[3]

---

[1] Tashi, independent celebrant.
[2] Such organizations include Civil Ceremonies Ltd (2002–), the Association of Independent Celebrants (2007–), the Fellowship of Professional Celebrants (2011–), the United Kingdom Society of Celebrants (2011–), the Fellowship of Independent Celebrants (2013–), and the Institute of Professional Celebrants (2018–).
[3] Stephanie Pywell (2020) 'The day of their dreams: celebrant-led wedding celebration ceremonies' 2 *Child and Family Law Quarterly* 177, 181.

Stories about independent celebrants and the ceremonies they conduct increasingly appear in the media.[4]

Our focus in this chapter is not on wedding celebrancy in general[5] or even on the reasons why couples might choose to have a celebrant-led ceremony,[6] but on the more specific question of whether such ceremonies are used to reflect the beliefs of the parties. That is a dimension that has not been explored in the literature to date. Previous research into celebrant-led ceremonies in England and Wales has focused primarily on those conducting the ceremonies, rather than the experiences of the couples themselves. In analyzing the various ceremonies described by her survey respondents, Pywell acknowledged that it could not be ascertained from their responses 'whether these ceremonies were seen as having religious or spiritual significance'.[7] Meanwhile, Maureen Baker and Vivienne Elizabeth's research into independent celebrants in New Zealand highlighted the role of these celebrants in the rise of personalized weddings, but portrayed such weddings as essentially non-religious.[8]

We first provide an example of a celebrant-led ceremony and then discuss how independent celebrants can be accommodated within the current legal framework. We then examine three different dimensions of the role of belief in ceremonies led by an independent celebrant: the beliefs of the celebrant, the beliefs of couples opting for celebrant-led ceremonies, and whether and how beliefs were reflected in celebrant-led ceremonies.

A celebrant-led ceremony

There is, by definition, no set form for a ceremony led by an independent celebrant. Instead, the focus is on tailoring the ceremony to the couple.

---

[4] See, for example, *Bride Magazine* (2022) 'The rise of independent wedding celebrants', 14 May: www.bridemagazine.co.uk/articles/the-rise-of-independent-wedding-celebrants; *BBC News Online* (2022) 'I found my dream job in retirement – marrying people', 25 May: www.bbc.co.uk/news/business-61520904

[5] For the most comprehensive discussion of the role and regulation of independent celebrants, see Pywell (2020) 'The day of their dreams' and (2020) 'Beyond beliefs: a proposal to give couples in England and Wales a real choice of marriage officiants' 3 *Child and Family Law Quarterly* 215.

[6] For discussion of the range of reasons why a couple might choose a ceremony led by an independent celebrant, see Rebecca Probert, Rajnaara C. Akhtar, and Sharon Blake (2022) *When Is a Wedding Not a Marriage? Exploring Non-legally Binding Marriage Ceremonies: Final Report* (Nuffield Foundation), 101–6.

[7] Pywell (2020) 'The day of their dreams', 190.

[8] Maureen Baker and Vivienne Elizabeth (2014) *Marriage in an Age of Cohabitation: How and When People Tie the Knot in the Twenty-first Century* (Oxford University Press), ch 4.

Celebrants explained that they would spend time getting to know the couple – through meetings, conversations, and questionnaires – and would write the ceremony specifically for that couple. As Dawn commented:

'The more you get to know them, the more you can personalize that and make it special. There's just something so wonderful … it's just a beautiful exciting time really, and you get really caught up in it all and come up with all these different things and help them choose. And I often find that a lot of couples don't always know what's available to them, and there's just so many beautiful additional parts you can add to ceremonies that make it special.'

In order to give a sense of what a ceremony led by an independent celebrant might look like, we draw here on Carla's account of the most recent ceremony she had conducted. The couple in question were Hindus and their (non-legally binding) Hindu wedding had taken place on approved premises, followed by their civil wedding at the same venue. However, the couple had wanted their ceremony to take place outside and so, as Carla explained, "we had the most beautiful celebrant ceremony out in the gardens, under a beautiful rose arch". What made this ceremony particularly special was how it was used to include the wider family of the bride and groom:

'I gave them the opportunity to include a symbolic ceremony within their wedding, and we decided that they are so family orientated and so really connected to all their families that we included a rose ceremony. Now, typically a rose ceremony includes the mothers or possibly the sisters of the bride and groom, and they come up and present a rose. So, when I said that they could include the female members of their families, what I didn't realize is that they were going to come back with 32 female members of their families that they wanted to include in the rose ceremony. Boy, what a spectacle that was! We had the bride's members of her family lined up down her side of the aisle, and the groom's down the other side. And the spectacle of colour with all the beautiful saris … they looked absolutely beautiful all of these lovely ladies. And then the groom presented a rose – a yellow rose to represent joy – to the bride's family … his gift to them. The bride gave an orange rose to the groom's … female members of his family, and then, two at a time from each side of the family, they came up, had a hug, and put their roses in the front. So, we had the biggest bouquet of orange and yellow roses at the end and it was just incredible. And then the bride and groom … they swapped their red roses and put those in. And they are still talking about it afterwards. They have all said that out of the whole week of weddings, that was the most joyous moment out of the whole week.'

Accommodating independent celebrants within the current legal framework

There is nothing in the Marriage Act 1949 to preclude independent celebrants working with registration officers to conduct weddings on approved premises, and a number of independent celebrants reported examples of such cooperation. One was a pilot scheme that had operated in Staffordshire offering 'combined ceremonies'; as Laura described, "the registrars would agree to be in the same room, at the same time – shock, horror! – as celebrants, so that both parts of the wedding ceremony could be conducted. Both the legal and the celebratory side".

Others gave examples of different elements of the ceremony taking place in different rooms to demarcate the legal and the celebratory. Deborah's most recent wedding had involved her starting the ceremony in one room; after the ring exchange, the couple "went out to another room to do the legal bits and pieces with the registrars and then they came back ... and we did a handfasting to complete". As she acknowledged, though, it "was unusual to have the registrars there at the same time". More typical was the experience of Anya, who was taken on to undertake the handfasting but performed it after the registration officers had left the premises.

The fact that both Deborah and Anya reported conducting a handfasting indicates that a collaboration between registration officers and independent celebrants may be particularly convenient where a particular ritual is not one that the former feel able to include within a civil wedding.[9] However, as Laura's explanation of combined ceremonies indicated, such collaborations were not particularly common. Other celebrants reported experiencing opposition from registration officers where a couple wanted to have their legal wedding and a celebrant-led ceremony on approved premises. Gaia commented that she had lost one booking because "the registrar flatly refused to conduct the ceremony if I was involved". Laura and Tashi also knew of couples who had been told that they could not have a celebrant at their ceremony, while others gave examples of

---

[9] On the bar on material that is 'religious in nature', see Stephanie Pywell and Rebecca Probert (2018) 'Neither sacred nor profane: the permitted content of civil marriage ceremonies' 30 *Child and Family Law Quarterly* 415. While registration officers may conduct an additional 'celebratory' ceremony that includes religious content – on which see Rebecca Probert (2021) *Tying the Knot: The Formation of Marriage 1836–2020* (Cambridge University Press), 247 – they may not have capacity to do so given the number of ceremonies they may be conducting in a single day.

registration services placing pressure on approved premises not to allow celebrant-led ceremonies.[10]

The role of belief in celebrant-led ceremonies
The beliefs of independent celebrants

The independent celebrants within our study held a range of different beliefs. While a number noted that they had no beliefs, others described themselves as Christian (including Anglican, Catholic, and Serbian Orthodox), Buddhist, Hindu, Humanist, Jewish, or Pagan. Since they were providing this information as part of a short form sent to them in advance of participating in a focus group, they did not have the same opportunity as our interviewees to provide details. Nonetheless, the subtleties and complexities of belief were reflected in answers such as 'non-practising Christian', 'Humanist/Spiritual' and 'Atheist/Pagan (it's complicated)'.

What united them was their view that their own beliefs were secondary to those of the couple. As Gaia put it: "I value all faiths. ... With my personal faith beliefs, I'm not what's important." A number of celebrants noted that while the ceremonies they conducted were in many respects similar to those conducted by Humanist celebrants, what differentiated them from Humanist celebrants was that they were not representing a single belief system. Jan explained that "with an independent celebrant, there are no set rules or etiquettes or traditions. Everything is compiled based on what the couple believes, whether that's religious, spiritual, or secular content or a mix of".

A few did note that sharing the same religious beliefs or cultural background as the couple could help them to fulfil the wishes of the couple. Jacob reported conducting a ceremony for a Christian bride and a Jewish groom who had wanted some Jewish elements incorporated: "Just so happens we're Jewish, so breaking the glass is not a problem. I put in some Hebrew prayers as well. Actually I sung in Hebrew and I spoke Hebrew, and it was totally bespoke and it was fantastic. So, they were very lucky!"

In that case, the fact that he shared the beliefs of the groom was purely serendipitous. Lakshmi, by contrast, specifically introduced herself as an "Asian female celebrant" and drew on her religious and cultural background in the ceremonies she conducted. As she explained, the concept of a celebrant was something of an alien one within Asian cultures. Her background enabled her to work with couples – and more significantly their families – to explain her role and reassure them that it

---

[10] See further Rebecca Probert, Rajnaara C. Akhtar, and Sharon Blake (2022), 91.

would not be "blasphemous" to have a ceremony that combined elements of religious traditions.

The beliefs of couples opting for celebrant-led ceremonies

Of those who had chosen a ceremony led by an independent celebrant, most simply said that neither they nor their spouses held any religious beliefs. However, this had not always been the case, with Lucy and Mairead both having held religious beliefs at an earlier stage in their lives: Lucy "used to be a Methodist many, many moons ago", while Mairead defined herself as "culturally Irish Catholic". In the few cases where interviewees did hold religious beliefs, these were not shared with their spouse: Karen summed up her current beliefs as "Christian, but not going to church a lot" and described her husband as "agnostic", while Sita, who described herself as Hindu but "not overly practising", referred to her husband as "more atheist", later adding that "he doesn't know anything about the faith and isn't really that interested". In addition, Amanda, who initially disclaimed having any religious beliefs, went on to describe herself as "probably erring on the Christian side" but "definitely not practising". When asked if her husband shared her beliefs, she expressed the view that he "is probably even less than what I am. Although he's perhaps a little bit more on the spiritual side. But he doesn't have any religious thoughts within him".

Unsurprisingly, then, most had not considered having a religious wedding. Chloe explained that she was not "anti" religion but added, "it's just not part of my identity. So, I wouldn't want it to be a part of any sort of ceremony that was part of my life". Vicky commented that the only person in her family who was "vaguely religious" was her mum, but added that "there was no pressure from her to get married in a church, because she would have known that that would have been just weird for us, like, quite hypocritical really. Well, not hypocritical but just a bit strange, sort of, making promises to God".

Sita also commented that it would be a "bit hypocritical" for her to "go into a temple and have a big Hindu ceremony". The only interviewee who had investigated the possibility of having a religious wedding was Mairead, who had thought of having a Catholic wedding to reflect her upbringing and earlier participation in Catholic rites; ultimately, however, she decided against this for a mix of personal and religious reasons.[11]

---

[11] As she noted, because she grew up Irish Catholic but her partner did not, a Catholic wedding would not be about them both; there were, in addition, complications in terms of what the Church required.

Similarly, when independent celebrants referred to the beliefs of the couples whose ceremonies they conducted, they primarily spoke of couples who did not share the same beliefs or couples who were not particularly religious and did not want a "full" religious wedding. Lakshmi, for example, saw herself as catering for "a younger generation, who are not so religious", while Sue reported conducting a ceremony for a Muslim couple who were "very Westernized" and did not want a "full" religious wedding.

This suggests that couples who hold religious beliefs are unlikely to consider a celebrant-led ceremony as a stand-alone alternative to a religious wedding if such a wedding is available to them.[12] Independent celebrants emphasized that they were catering for couples who did not wish to have a religious wedding but at the same time wanted something more than what was offered in a civil wedding. As Rob commented, "more and more people are turning away from the Church, but they don't want this completely sterile, almost irreligious service at the registry office". While he and other celebrants had a somewhat exaggerated view of the strictness of the prohibition on religious content,[13] many of the rituals that had been included in a celebrant-led ceremony would not have been permitted in a civil wedding.[14]

On occasion, however, the celebrant-led ceremony was in *addition* to a religious wedding or ceremony. Jan reported coordinating the "weekend celebration" of a couple whose religious wedding in their local church was followed by a weekend of glamping and a bigger ceremony. As she explained, the bride "had grown up in a religious family with a religious background" and "had a commitment to her values and beliefs and that side and her family", but "didn't want that to be the focus of the day". And Carla, who, as already mentioned, had conducted a ceremony for a Hindu couple who had a whole sequence of ceremonies, noted that "they

---

[12] There are, of course, many couples who hold strong religious beliefs but will not be able to marry in a way that reflects those beliefs. This is a particular issue for same-sex couples see Paul Johnson, Robert M. Vanderbeck, and Silvia Falcetta (2017) *Religious Marriage of Same-sex Couples: A Report on Places of Worship in England and Wales Registered for the Solemnization of Same-sex Marriage* (University of York and University of Leeds) – and also for couples with different beliefs, as discussed in Chapter 5.

[13] Rob commented, "as far as I'm aware ... the music can't really mention anything spiritual or anything with God or anything like that. Even if it's a secular song, you can't have any kind of vaguely religious music". In fact, incidental religious references have been permitted since 2005: The Marriages and Civil Partnerships (Approved Premises) Regulations 2005, SI 2005/3168, Sch 2, para 11(2).

[14] On this, see Pywell and Probert (2018); see also Pywell (2020) 'The day of their dreams', 190–4.

are all recommending me to their Asian friends who want a celebrant wedding after their Hindu wedding". This suggests that this combination of ceremonies was not unique.

Reflecting beliefs in celebrant-led ceremonies

Among our interviewees, none reported including words or rituals that were both exclusively religious and explicitly linked to their own religious beliefs. Karen, for example, had a handfasting but did not appear to regard this as a specifically religious practice, although she was aware that it would not have been permitted in a civil wedding.[15] Similarly, while Lucy reported jumping the broomstick and described this as "Pagan",[16] for her, "it was just a bit of fun, really, for everyone". A more serious element within her ceremony was the lighting of candles in memory of both her mother and her husband's father because they "wanted them to be present in spirit", although she immediately added, "I know that sounds really weird when you're not religious".

Instead, interviewees described ceremonies that had included religious elements in a more subtle way. Such elements were of religious significance to them but would not necessarily be seen by others as religious in nature. For Sita, for example, the inclusion of candles was a means of acknowledging her Hindu faith. As she explained:

'So with Hinduism, light and a candle is really important because for Diwali, it's a celebration of light and moving darkness away. So, what we had asked the celebrant to do is, when people were coming into the barn, they all had a candle to light. And then, once they come into the barn, there was like an A-frame and everybody would put their lit candle on the A-frame and then we ... [my husband] and I were together at the front ... we then lit our own candle, which was bigger, and put it in the middle to just symbolize, you know, the part of Hinduism that it links to. And also we're bringing light together and brightness into our lives. So, we kind of like did small things like that.'

---

[15] She noted that in her role as a celebrant, she had conducted a ceremony for a couple who wanted a handfasting but couldn't "because it was said to be Pagan". Anya also described being brought in to conduct a handfasting where a couple had initially been offered one by a registrar "as part of the ceremony" but another registrar had subsequently objected on the basis that it was religious and Pagan.

[16] There are, it should be noted, multiple origin stories for broomstick weddings. For an analysis of the concept, see Rebecca Probert (2005) 'Chinese whispers and Welsh weddings' 20 *Continuity and Change* 211.

In addition, Mairead had welcomed the opportunity to include a "nod" to her Irish Catholic upbringing by incorporating a ritual that involved drinking from a ceremonial quaich cup:

'I knew we weren't going to have a religious ceremony, because like I said, we're not very religious, but I always had in the back of my mind, oh, but I was brought up with this as a kid, and I sort of thought it'd be nice to bring in something that almost has a bit of an, almost a little bit of a religious feel, or a little bit of a ritualistic kind of feel, like it had a ritual kind of quality to it, like pouring a bit of drink in and then taking a sip from it. It felt like a little nod to my Irish Catholic upbringing.'

In a similar vein, no celebrants described conducting an entirely religious ceremony. While Bethany, Kester, Laura, Mel, and Tashi had all conducted handfastings, none specifically ascribed any specifically religious significance to that. Including rituals that reflected religious beliefs was important for those who held beliefs but were not practising or those who held spiritual beliefs which were not reflected in formalized religions. Sue, for example, had conducted a ceremony for a Muslim couple who had wanted "some Muslim elements" in their ceremony:

'At the end of the ceremony, they did what's called a *sapatia*, where they smash clay pots that are decorated with gold and full of symbolic elements. So, silver for wealth, beans for prosperity. So, there was a very symbolic element, which they place on the floor and they smash with their heels, and the theory is whoever smashes it first rules the household. So, there's a competition to smash it first. But it's all good fun. So, it was important that they had ... they could include those elements without it being a full religious ceremony, which is why they chose the celebrant.'

While none of our interviewees referred to including religious elements to reflect the beliefs of their family members, some celebrants gave examples of couples who had done so. Barbara recalled conducting a ceremony for a bride who was not religious but whose father was a Nigerian pastor; she explained, "as an independent celebrant, I was able to bring the religious elements in to please her family, which she wanted included". Bethany commented that people might "want their dad to do a Bible reading because it's an important part of getting him to be part of the wedding, whereas he wants them to marry in church".

Others reported that their ceremonies were designed to respect religious differences. Rather than directly incorporating a specific religious element, they worked to create something new. Lakshmi spoke of "translating" and "blending" traditional religious elements, giving the example of couples saying their "personal vows" to each other while walking round the fire four times instead of the recitation of the scriptures that would accompany this in a traditional Hindu ceremony. Similarly, Bethany referred to "making a new tradition of marriage" for interfaith couples.

All these different challenges were reflected in the ceremony that Kester conducted for a couple who did not share the same beliefs as each other or their families. As he described, the husband "was a Pagan of the northern tradition", while the wife "had been brought up to be vaguely agnostic, a little bit on the atheistic side but was sort of spiritually curious". However, both came from families "with very, very strict fundamentalist Christian elements in them". As a result, he had to design a ceremony that would incorporate northern Pagan traditions and symbols, mean something "deeply spiritually satisfying to the couple involved", and not offend their relations. He achieved this by creating a sound circle. As he commented:

> 'You can't do that in a single faith ceremony, and you can't do that in a civil ceremony. The only people who can do that ... the only ones who would even attempt to do that are celebrants. And that's one of the reasons why we're important. Because we do take what people want ... take what has meaning to our couples and their families and their communities and their wider context and put that into a short, beautiful ceremony that is relatable on a series of levels.'

Conclusion

Personalization is clearly a key element of celebrant-led ceremonies. But such personalization should not necessarily be linked to consumerism or commercialization. The ceremonial choices made by those opting for a celebrant-led ceremony reflected a need for internal validity through authentic individual expression and external validity through social legitimization. For those who came from a religious background but no longer subscribed fully to the formal beliefs they were raised with, or those who defined themselves as believing but no longer practising, including some acknowledgement of their religious heritage or beliefs in their celebrant-led ceremony allowed them to express this part of their identity without the hypocrisy that they felt a full religious wedding would bring.

Our evidence therefore suggests that independent celebrants play a valuable role in catering for such couples. Commenting on the Law Commission's then-provisional proposals for reform, the Association of Independent Celebrants made the case that including independent celebrants in any future reform would be necessary to reflect the principles of fairness and equality, respecting individuals' wishes and beliefs and increasing the range of choices available to couples.[17] While organizations such as the OneSpirit Interfaith Foundation (discussed in Chapter 5) or Humanists UK (discussed in Chapter 7) are willing to cater for couples who hold beliefs which do not fit within any formal system, such couples may not feel comfortable aligning themselves with the values of a specific formalized organization.

Under the Law Commission's scheme, independent celebrants would, if enabled by the government, be able to apply individually to the General Register Office to be authorized, rather than being nominated by an organization. While this model has been criticized by some commentators,[18] it has been largely welcomed by independent celebrants.[19] We do not think that independent celebrants would wish to align themselves with a specific set of beliefs; that, after all, would run counter to their willingness to embrace *different* beliefs. As the Association of Independent Celebrants pointed out, '[a]s independent celebrants we can design ceremonies unique to each couple's beliefs, backgrounds and values'.[20]

One limitation of the Law Commission's scheme is that independent officiants would only be authorized to officiate at civil weddings. However, the Law Commission also recommends that it should be possible for civil weddings to include more explicitly religious content. Within our study, the examples of elements of religion being included in celebrant-led ceremonies could largely have been accommodated within a wedding that was still recognizably a 'civil' one. In the view of Kester, the proposed reforms would be: "An absolutely massive step towards equality, because it wouldn't matter to a certain extent what you look like, what colour you were, what creed you were, what variant of that. A celebrant, somewhere, will get you, and so someone will get you right."

---

[17] See, for example, Association of Independent Celebrants (2021) *Licensing Independent Wedding Celebrants: A Proposed Role for Independent Celebrants in Future Wedding Law Reform* (Association of Independent Celebrants).

[18] Russell Sandberg (2021) *Religion and Marriage Law: The Need for Reform* (Bristol University Press), 80–1.

[19] See, for example, Association of Independent Celebrants (2021).

[20] Association of Independent Celebrants (2021), 5.

9

Ceremonies Led by Friends and Family

'It was about having somebody there that really knew us, got us and wanted to join us in the next stage of our life'[1]

Introduction

In this penultimate chapter, we focus on those who want a friend or family member to conduct their ceremony.

A number of examples of this trend were reported in our study by both interviewees and those involved in conducting ceremonies. In some cases, the person who had been asked to lead the ceremony already had experience in conducting ceremonies. In other cases, the friend or family member performed the ceremony as a one-off favour for the couple. In that sense, these were the ultimate personalized ceremonies in that the celebrant, as well as the ceremony, was unique to the couple.

The issue of ceremonies being led by family and friends is not one that has attracted much attention to date in England and Wales.[2] We first look at the range of ceremonies led by family and friends. In certain cases, having a friend or family member lead the ceremony enabled the couple to have

---

[1] Amanda, reporting how she wanted a celebrant she knew to conduct her ceremony.

[2] It is, however, already an established practice in the United States: *The Times*, reporting on the Law Commission's recommendations, noted that in 2018 'almost a third of all weddings in the US were conducted by a friend or relative, who was "ordained" to officiate by a recognized body': *The Times* (2022) 'Say "I do" beside the seaside with plan to relax wedding rules', 19 July. See also Rainesford Stauffer (2019) 'Why more couples are getting married by a friend' *The Atlantic* 10 April: www.theatlantic.com/family/arch ive/2019/04/more-couples-having-friends-officiate-their-weddings/586750/ See further the discussion of the role of the Universal Life Church (in the section 'By the power vested in me …') in this regard.

a ceremony that aligned with their religious beliefs in a way that might not otherwise have been possible.

By definition, those who perform ceremonies as a one-off are not going to be among those campaigning for legal recognition. And while those friends or family members who had already performed ceremonies for other couples might be willing to become authorized as officiants (assuming that option is open to them), it is less likely that individuals would wish (or even be able) to be authorized to perform a single wedding. As we shall show, however, the Law Commission's recommendations do accommodate the possibility of a legal wedding being led by a friend or family member.

The range of ceremonies led by family and friends

In a few cases, it was a family member who had led the ceremony. Where a particular family member already had some experience of conducting ceremonies for other couples, it was natural for them to be asked: Ellis' brother was a deacon, while Polly's eldest brother had conducted ceremonies "for other friends abroad". As she explained, though, her ceremony was actually led by *both* of her brothers: "As soon as I mentioned to my other brother that I was thinking of asking my oldest brother … he was like, 'what about me?' So, I was, 'great. Do it together. That's nice'."

In addition, Amal's *nikah* was conducted at home by her father. While the arrangements for that ceremony were influenced by its timing – it took place while COVID-19 restrictions were in force – there is in fact no need for a *nikah* to be performed by an imam. Other interviewees had also contemplated asking a family member to conduct their *nikah*.

However, asking a friend to lead the ceremony was more common.[3] Again, in some cases the friend in question had a professional involvement in conducting ceremonies. Darain and Nadia both had their *nikahs* conducted by imams who they described as friends; as the latter commented, "he sort of knew our backgrounds and stuff, so the prayers made were really personal to us". Peter had been "able to call on a priest friend" to conduct a ceremony for him and his husband. Stella, who was an interfaith minister, had asked a friend who was also an interfaith minister to conduct her ceremony. Friendship had also played a role when interviewees were choosing an independent celebrant to lead their ceremony. Lucy had asked a fellow celebrant who was "a dear friend", while Amanda, who worked for an independent celebrant, had wanted her ceremony to be conducted by her

---

[3]   Our focus here is on those who were already friends rather than on friendships forged as a result of being involved in conducting a couple's ceremony (a common theme within our focus groups with Humanist and independent celebrants).

boss, who she described as having been a "huge part" of her life and career and "like a mother figure" to her.[4] As she explained, this link:

> 'just made it easier for us to be able to talk about what we wanted without someone thinking that we were mad and crazy. And someone that just got it and understood the angle that we were coming from. We just wanted it … to make it really personal, the wording that we wanted to use, to include our guests in it and his children, my stepchildren, as well.'

In other cases, the friend was someone who had not previously conducted ceremonies. As we saw in Chapter 6, this was particularly common among those choosing a Pagan ceremony. There were also a few interviewees who described themselves as having no beliefs and who had asked a friend to lead their ceremony as a one-off because they judged that particular friend would do a good job. For Orla, it was a matter of reviewing their respective friends to assess who had "the right mix of, you know, good speaking voice, won't make inappropriate jokes, and would be willing to do it". Aidan had deliberately chosen "someone that we didn't know that well but we trusted to do a good job and to do a thorough job", and Daisy had opted for a "very amusing" friend. In each case, the choice reflected the specific role that they wanted their friend to perform.

Understanding and enabling beliefs

For some, choosing a friend or family member to conduct their wedding ceremony was a way of ensuring that their religious beliefs were understood and shared. Grainne laid particular emphasis on the importance of this. As she explained, "I could have gone and got a Humanist or somebody, but I didn't … I wanted somebody who understood the religion, belief system that I participate in".

Similarly, for Ellis and Emma, having someone who knew them conduct the ceremony ensured a level of awareness of, and sensitivity to, Ellis' complex view of Christianity and Emma's lack of religious beliefs. Ellis came from a family in which religion played a very significant part: as she explained, she had been "involved in the church as a youth group leader for a long time and I played in a worship band and things like that before I came out", and her parents and her brother were all involved in their Christian church as deacons. They had asked her brother to lead the ceremony. Ellis noted that

---

[4]   Within the focus groups, Ruth, an independent celebrant, also reported conducting a ceremony for her best friend.

while her brother primarily had experience in leading wedding ceremonies that were "all very Christian church focused", he had put together something slightly different for them; she added, "I didn't even have to ask him to tone it down or anything. He just knew what to do". Emma was similarly full of praise for the way the ceremony had been crafted: "It highlighted parts of your faith and Christianity and that kind of weaved into our life together."

While their beliefs differed, both felt that it was very important for their ceremony to have a faith element. For Ellis, it was a means of connecting to her faith:

'Whilst I'm not a practising Christian any more in that way, it still holds a lot of meaning to me because, for me, my understanding of love comes from Christianity, basically. Not as religion necessarily teaches ... love is an unconditional nonjudgemental thing comes from my growing up in a Christian space.'

Emma, meanwhile, explained that having a religious element to the ceremony was a way of demonstrating to Ellis' family that she respected her new spouse's faith: "It was nice for your parents to see that whilst I am not religious, I respect and understand that you are and that that's important to you, and so important that I even have it on my wedding day, because we are getting married, the two of us."

For this couple, the religious ceremony had an additional significance. As Emma explained, Ellis' brother's participation was an important signal of acceptance:

'Having that support in that he wanted to do that for us, for our wedding was very meaningful to me, particularly because I wasn't sure ... going into a very religious family and seeing that, you always wonder how that's going to go and if they really do support you authentically, because of their beliefs and because you're aware of how some people react to your sexuality because of that religion. It felt like an additional acceptance as well and validation as well, which was really, really nice. So, that's why I liked it so much, that he did that because it was like, okay, he really does support us and therefore the entire family does too.'

Having Ellis' brother conduct the ceremony also meant that the couple did not need to look externally for a celebrant who would conduct a religious ceremony for them. While this was not a point they raised, its significance is apparent from a recent empirical study of same-sex couples who had had a religious wedding. This study noted the particular challenges such couples face given the limited number of places of worship that are registered for same-sex weddings, with some participants experiencing 'uncertainties, stresses, and anxieties about approaching places of worship where they feared there was a chance of encountering hostility'.[5]

The reluctance of many religious groups to conduct same-sex weddings and the consequent importance of the role played by friends and family in enabling same-sex couples to have a religious wedding ceremony also emerged in other accounts. Peter noted that his religious ceremony, conducted by a friend who was a Catholic priest, "had to be slightly below the radar because it's not approved of in the Catholic Church". John, a Catholic priest, similarly explained that he had "blessed the marriage of a same-sex couple who are friends of mine, following the civil ceremony". This too had been strictly unofficial, and he had been keen for it not to become public knowledge – "you know, no photographs on Facebook or anything like that"; he and the other two priests present had not been there "with the knowledge of any of our bishops, of course".

'By the power vested in me ...'

In the United States, if a couple want a friend or family member to conduct their wedding, there is the option of that person being ordained as a minister. A key role here is played by the Universal Life Church.[6] According to Dusty Hoesly, himself a minister within the church, the Universal Life Church will 'ordain anyone nearly instantly', regardless of whether they hold religious beliefs, and its weddings can be entirely personal to the couple.[7] Of the 20 million ministers the Universal Life Church has ordained since its foundation in 1962, it has been estimated that around 80–90 per cent became ordained in order to conduct weddings for family or friends.[8] As Hoesly noted, the experience of the Universal

---

[5]   Silvia Falcetta, Paul Johnson, and Robert M. Vanderbeck (2021) 'The experience of religious same-sex marriage in England and Wales: understanding the opportunities and limits created by the Marriage (Same Sex Couples) Act 2013' 35 *International Journal of Law, Policy and the Family* ebab003: https://doi.org/10.1093/lawfam/ebab003.

[6]   For discussion of the Universal Life Church and the questions over the status of the ceremonies conducted by its ministers, see Robert E. Rains (2010) 'Marriage in the time of internet ministers: I now pronounce you married, but who am I do to so?' 14 *Journal of Internet Law* 10.

[7]   Dusty Hoesly (2017) 'Your wedding, your way: personalized, nonreligious weddings through the Universal Life Church' in Ryan T. Cragun, Christel Manning, and Lori L. Fazzino (eds) *Organized Secularism in the United States: New Directions in Research* (De Gruyter), 253.

[8]   Dusty Hoesly (2015) '"Need a minister? How about your brother?": The Universal Life Church between religion and non-religion' 4 *Secularism and Nonreligion* Art 12: http://doi.org/10.5334/snr.be

Life Church 'shows how many avowedly secular people take up a strategic religious identity in order to achieve a desired nonreligious ritual in an individualized manner'.[9]

Within England and Wales, there has not been the same scope to become ordained purely for the purpose of conducting a legal wedding. With the exception of the Church of England and the Church in Wales (both of which have demanding procedures for ordination), being a minister confers no right to solemnize a legal wedding. Nor is it likely that the Law Commission's scheme would lead to individuals becoming authorized as an officiant simply to conduct the legal wedding of a friend or family member. Belief officiants will need to be nominated by a religious or non-religious belief organization, and both they and independent officiants will need to undertake training in the role. That said, if there is the option of being authorized as an independent celebrant, then it would at least be *possible* for a friend or family member to be able to officiate at a wedding.

As Hoesley made clear, one of the reasons for the popularity of strategic ordinations via the Universal Life Church in the United States is the limited options available for couples to have a non-religious ceremony. There may therefore be less demand in England and Wales for family and friends to lead the ceremony given the greater range of options for non-religious couples to have a legal wedding that is meaningful to them. Even under the current law, civil weddings conducted by registrars can take place in a wide range of locations, and under the Law Commission's scheme the remaining restrictions on location will vanish. Moreover, if the Law Commission's scheme is implemented in full, couples will also have the option of a civil ceremony officiated by an independent officiant or a belief wedding officiated by an officiant nominated by a non-religious belief organization. As we have seen in Chapters 7 and 8, both Humanist and independent celebrants laid considerable importance on getting to know the couples they were marrying in advance of the ceremony.

That said, there were individuals whose preference would still have been for a friend to conduct their ceremony. Grainne, for example, expressed the view that even having a "licensed Druid" conduct the ceremony would not have been as nice for her as having these "two very special people do it". Aidan similarly reflected:

'If the law was that we could have got married in that venue, we probably would have got an official celebrant who had that legal power. In retrospect, we really enjoyed the way we did it, because he was someone who meant something to us. He was doing what we

---

[9] Hoesly (2015), 253.

considered the important bit, the exchanging of the vows and the rings and the blessing, if you like. So, it felt more real doing it the way we did.'

For those who specifically want a friend or family member to conduct the ceremony, it should be noted that it will not be necessary for that person to be an officiant in order to do so. The role of an officiant is to ensure that the parties freely express consent to marry each other, that the other requirements of the ceremony are met, and that the relevant documentation is signed.[10] While officiants may, and often will, also conduct the ceremony, there is no requirement for them to do so. The simplest way for a friend or family member to conduct a legally recognized wedding ceremony would therefore be for them to work in conjunction with an authorized officiant.[11] Such a solution enables couples to be married by someone they know while also ensuring that the ceremony complies with the requirements for a legal wedding.

Conclusion

Choosing a friend or family member to conduct one's wedding might seem far removed from the idea of a wedding conducted by a religious authority figure. Yet there are some important similarities. After all, the law governing weddings in England and Wales has its roots in the localism of the Anglican parish system. Anglican clergy would have been familiar figures, responsible for conducting the key rites of passage for their parishioners. Similarly, among the participants in our study, those who had chosen a friend or family member to lead the ceremony were not alone in stressing the importance of knowing the person who was to conduct their wedding. In a number of cases, there was a long pre-existing relationship with the person who conducted the ceremony: Ajey and Arun emphasized how long they or their spouse had known their priest; Farid explained that he had chosen a *nikah* with a sheikh who he and his wife "respect a lot"; and Sarah noted that "it was always going to actually be my minister ... doing the Christian ceremony". Others had built a relationship with the person who was to conduct the ceremony prior to it taking place: Mairead, for example, had chosen an independent celebrant to conduct a non-legally binding ceremony

---

[10] Law Commission (2022) *Celebrating Marriage: A New Weddings Law* (19 July), para 4.63.

[11] Among the celebrants we spoke to, Christine indicated that she would be happy to oversee the legal side if the couple wanted a friend or member of the family to conduct their ceremony. However, most celebrants saw their role as leading the ceremony, and while they were keen to involve friends and family, they had some reservations about them leading the ceremony. As Laura put it, "whilst it might be a lovely notion to have a family friend do it ... it can often go disastrously wrong".

on approved premises rather than booking a registrar, because she and her husband had felt "quite anxious" about only meeting the person who was to conduct their ceremony a few minutes in advance. While interviewees were generally full of praise for the registrars who had conducted their legal wedding, they had had no say in *which* registration officers did so. As Hazel noted, "it felt like we were just going to this person who gets to decide who we are and how we are, which felt really weird".

Under the Law Commission's scheme, family and friends would be able to work with officiants to lead legal weddings. Alternatively, if couples specifically want to separate the legal wedding or to have a religious ceremony which would not currently be possible due to the exemptions from equality law that apply to religious groups, they could still have a friend/family-led non-legally binding ceremony which reflects their beliefs.

10

Conclusion

Introduction

As we have shown, the Marriage Act 1836 was intended to enable couples to marry in accordance with their beliefs. But its successor, the Marriage Act 1949, no longer achieves this, partly because of legal changes that have limited its original flexibility, but mainly because of the huge changes in the composition of society since 1836. The apparent neutrality of key regulations within the current law masks considerable inequality in practice: put simply, rules constructed for and around Christian ceremonies are easier for Christian weddings to satisfy. And the law makes no provision for those who are of different faiths, those who worship outdoors, those who hold non-religious beliefs such as Humanism, and those who want a ceremony that includes religious elements but not a full religious service. The recommendations put forward by the Law Commission in *Celebrating Marriage* will, if implemented, enable more couples to make their legal commitment to each other in a way that reflects their beliefs. In this concluding chapter, we draw together the evidence to show why that is important.

To do so, we return to the question posed by Jane Mair about the nature of religious marriage that we discussed in Chapter 1. First, we reflect on whether religious weddings are simply a historical 'remnant' in the sense of being motivated by tradition rather than by the beliefs of the parties. Second, we consider the importance of being able to satisfy legal and faith commitments in a single ceremony, especially where the alternative is a religious-only marriage. Third, we discuss how enabling couples to marry in accordance with their beliefs sends a message about respect, equality, and inclusion, and gives additional weight and meaning to the vows being made. Here, we broaden our frame of reference beyond the formal religious or non-religious belief systems on which we have primarily focused. Reflecting our findings that a number of people hold beliefs but are not practising, while others tick 'none' when asked about religious beliefs but still hold spiritual beliefs, we also discuss how their beliefs and values can be reflected in a legally recognized wedding.

In making these arguments, we are not intending to suggest that marriage itself should be privileged over other family forms. While our focus has been on belief in marriage, we think that it is important for civil partnerships to remain available as an alternative for those who are ideologically opposed to marriage but still wish for their relationship to be formally recognized by the state. At the same time, we disagree with those who argue that the law should *only* recognize either civil marriage or civil partnerships and that religious (or belief) marriage should be a purely private matter.[1] In our view, the way forward is for the law to be reformed so that it better recognizes the diverse beliefs and practices through which couples in contemporary society see themselves as getting married.[2]

The continuing importance of belief weddings

Across our study, we had many individuals who described their beliefs as being central to their lives and for whom being able to marry in accordance with those beliefs was correspondingly crucial. This was the case across a variety of different belief systems and regardless of the legal status of the wedding. For example, Sarah explained that for her, being able to marry with Christian vows and prayers was important because:

> 'For me, being a Christian, that is the most important thing in my life and that's how I suppose I understand what it means for me to be a person. ... And that's how I understand marriage. My understanding of what it means to me to be married is to live in accordance with something that God has given us, and marriage, ultimately, I believe is an institution created by God. Though obviously recognized by the state.'

Manizeh similarly explained that "because Zoroastrianism is an important part of my life, it was important to have that religious ceremony, because that's what I counted as the marriage". Aashvi, whose Hindu ceremony

---

[1] See, for example, Tamara Metz (2004) 'Why we should disestablish marriage' in Mary Lyndon Shanley (ed) *Just Marriage* (Oxford University Press), 100; Lawrence G. Torcello (2008) 'Is the state endorsement of any marriage justifiable? Same-sex marriage, civil unions, and the marriage privatization model' 22 *Public Affairs Quarterly* 43.

[2] For similar arguments about the importance of acknowledging and accommodating different views and practices, see Scot Peterson and Iain McLean (2013) *Legally Married: Love and Law in the UK and the US* (Edinburgh University Press); John Eekelaar (2013) 'Marriage: a modest proposal' 43 *Family Law* 83.

had taken place on the Ganges river, spoke of how important her Hindu roots were: "We didn't just do it for our grandparents; we did it for us." For many Muslim participants too, a *nikah* was integral to their beliefs, as without it they would not regard themselves as married. As Atif put it, "the most important thing is to be married in the eyes of God with the *nikah*". Indeed, a number emphasized that it was not a matter of 'choosing' to have a *nikah*, since the alternative of *not* having a *nikah* was unthinkable for them. The *nikah* marked the point at which couples felt able to engage in an intimate relationship, whether it occurred before or after the legal wedding.[3]

It should be noted that holding particular beliefs did not mean couples simply accepted that a wedding had to be performed in a particular way. A common theme across our sample was active reflection on, rather than passive adherence to, traditional wedding forms – personalization rather than prescription. As discussed in Chapter 4, where language or rituals were seen as reflecting values to which couples did not subscribe, they negotiated with those conducting the ceremony to choose the ceremonial elements they saw as best fitting their beliefs and their relationships. Jasmine, for example, noted that she had wanted certain things taken out of her Jain wedding "because they're not relevant in this day and age".

Satisfying legal and belief commitments

Across our study, most of those who had a ceremony conducted in accordance with prescribed religious rites saw that as the point at which they were married, regardless of whether it came before or after a legal wedding and regardless also of their religion. Thus, Abir described how having a *nikah* meant "that was us classed as married"; Jasmine referred to her Hindu wedding as being "the day I got married", although her legal wedding had taken place a week earlier; and Sarah didn't consider herself married until her Christian ceremony was carried out, even though her legal wedding had also taken place in a church. Similarly, Tara, reflecting on her own Buddhist wedding, commented:

'My real wedding was the one that was my Buddhist wedding, because that's my whole ... that's my daily life, my Buddhist practice and, you know, it's the glasses through which I view the world, and I would

---

[3] For further discussion of how for the majority of Muslim participants, the *nikah* marked the start of any kind of intimacy, see Rebecca Probert, Rajnaara C. Akhtar, and Sharon Blake (2022) *When Is a Wedding Not a Marriage? Exploring Non-legally Binding Marriage Ceremonies: Final Report* (Nuffield Foundation), 67–8.

not have considered myself married, even with that official bit of paper, without the Buddhist wedding.'

Many of those whose ceremony had been conducted by a Humanist or independent celebrant were also clear that this was their 'real' wedding. Linda, for example, commented that "we were very firm that our proper wedding was going to be the Humanist ceremony with all our friends and family there", and Mairead similarly felt that her celebrant-led ceremony "was the most meaningful because it felt like this is our wedding".

The corollary of this was that the legal wedding was not the 'real' wedding, particularly where it took the form of a civil wedding in a register office. For some, this sense of unreality was exacerbated by the fact that the form of a civil wedding was unfamiliar to them: Darain, for example, commented that "it was not really like a wedding". For others, like May, it was because the civil wedding had "nothing to do with us as people or as individuals or anything like that". Grainne was similarly baffled as to why the law attached particular significance to "just saying two phrases" as compared to the promises that they had made in their other ceremony, commenting that "none of it makes sense, quite honestly".

As a result, having to have a separate civil wedding was simply an unwelcome bureaucratic process for many participants. For Amanda, Karim, and Mairead, it was "the paperwork"; Chloe and Stella both described it as a "tick-box exercise"; Uma thought it was just "crossing the t's [and] dotting the i's"; and May dismissed it as "just a cold, legal bit of red tape". This view was shared by many interviewees, regardless of whether the civil wedding came before or after their other ceremony and regardless of their particular beliefs. That said, among those whose religious ceremony had already taken place, there was an additional sense of weariness at the duplication of effort involved. As Laila explained, the civil wedding "didn't hold any significance. It didn't hold any meaning, and when we went through the steps, it just felt very formal and I just want to sign a paper and get done with it because I've already done what I needed to do". The idea of being able to satisfy legal and belief commitments in a single ceremony was accordingly welcomed by the vast majority of our participants as not only easier but also cheaper.[4]

---

[4] The assumption that it is simple and cheap to have a separate register office wedding is not borne out by the evidence. In principle, it should be possible for a couple to get married in a register office in England or Wales for just £127. This fee is set by statute and comprises £35 per person for giving notice, £46 for the ceremony, and £11 for the certificate. However, the 'in principle' qualification is an important one. Research by Stephanie Pywell suggests that couples in about one third of local authority areas in England and Wales cannot marry for the £127 that the law prescribes because of the imposition of additional non-optional fees: Stephanie Pywell (2020) '2 + 2 = £127, if

In particular, our findings suggest that the majority of those whose religious ceremony had taken place before their legal wedding – and at least some of those who were in a religious-only marriage at the time of the interview[5] – would have had a single legal wedding if they had felt they were able to do so in a way that reflected their beliefs. Kiran, whose *nikah* had taken place seven or eight months before her register office wedding, noted that her preference would have been to do both on the same day. Similarly, Laila, whose illness had meant that her legal wedding was delayed, commented that having a single ceremony would have removed the worry of organizing a second event: "If the *nikah* and the civil ceremony could have just been one event, I would have just had one event." And Eda commented:

> 'The fact that we can give notice and have whatever ceremony and it would be legally binding, I think that's the main thing. It would just save a lot of additional work to get something done afterwards. Especially for people like myself, cos I consider myself married now, so really for me, what's the rush of trying to get something done as a formality, if that makes sense?'

The possibility of having a combined ceremony was also seen as making it harder for those who had no intention of being legally married to deceive someone into going through a religious ceremony by making promises that a legal wedding would follow. As Amina pointed out, if the option of a combined wedding was immediately available, then it would raise suspicion if someone said that they did not want that option: "I can't imagine how people could say 'Oh no, we won't do that option. Let's do the one where you have no protection'."

As we have discussed in earlier chapters, some religious groups do not have celebrants who officiate at weddings. But that would not preclude those wishing to be married according to the rites of such groups from having a

---

you're lucky' *Law Society Gazette* 3 March. In addition, there has been a massive diminution in the availability of register office weddings, with many former register offices having been transformed into 'approved premises' and charging higher fees, and limited slots for the basic statutory ceremony: Rebecca Probert, Stephanie Pywell, Rajnaara C. Akhtar, Sharon Blake, Tania Barton, and Vishal Vora (2022) 'Trying to get a piece of paper from City Hall? The availability, accessibility, and administration of the register office wedding' 44 *Journal of Social Welfare and Family Law* 226.

[5] It should be noted that there will always be some couples who wish to have a religious-only ceremony first – for example, to enable them to get to know each other better in advance of entering into a legal commitment; equally, there will also be couples who regard the religious-only ceremony as sufficient and do not see the need for a legal wedding at all: see further Rajnaara C. Akhtar, Patrick Nash, and Rebecca Probert (eds) (2020) *Cohabitation and Religious Marriage: Status, Similarities and Solutions* (Bristol University Press).

ceremony that satisfied both legal and belief commitments. Under the Law Commission's recommendations, an officiant does not have to lead the ceremony or require legally prescribed words to be said. It is hoped that the recommendations will make it easier for couples to approach an officiant to attend their ceremony discreetly to allow the couple's chosen ceremony to be legally recognized.

The expressive function of family law

Family law can perform an expressive function in different ways. At an institutional level, it can express the wider values of the legal system. At an individual level, it can provide a framework for couples themselves to express their beliefs and values.

At an institutional level, the legal options for getting married convey messages about the role of the state and of religion (or, more usually, specific religions). What is either required or permitted by the law matters. As Masha Antokolskaia has noted, having a system whereby there are both civil and religious routes for entry into marriage 'could be attributed to respect for pluralism and religious tolerance'.[6] However, she suggests that there are certain preconditions for regarding such a system as modern and democratic – no one dominant religion should be privileged to the detriment of others and there must be 'uniform, State-determined, minimal preconditions for the celebration of both civil and religious marriage'.[7]

We have shown in earlier chapters that our participants (quite justifiably) saw the law as privileging Christian weddings. No one thought that this privilege should be maintained given the diversity of religions and beliefs in modern-day England and Wales. As Linda commented, a choice between a civil wedding and a Christian one "just doesn't reflect the reality of England today". Participants accordingly welcomed the idea of being able to have a ceremony that both accorded with their beliefs and was given legal recognition as signalling respect, equality, and inclusion.[8] Dania commented that the recognition of other religious ceremonies "would just help you feel more integrated in society". As Amina summed up, "it's more fair and it's more religious and it's more inclusive for every ceremony and every kind of belief that people have in terms of how to get married".

---

[6]   Masha Antokolskaia (2006) *Harmonisation of Family Law in Europe: A Historical Perspective – A Tale of Two Millenia* (Intersentia), 301.

[7]   Masha Antokolskaia (2006), 301.

[8]   See, for example, the comments of Arun (Chapter 4), Dawn (Chapter 6), Shelley (Chapter 7), and Kester (Chapter 8)

The Law Commission's scheme, it should be noted, does not go so far as to confer recognition on *every* kind of belief. The kinds of organization that will be able to nominate officiants will need to reflect a section of the community rather than the beliefs of a single individual: a nominating organization will have to have members from at least 20 households 'who meet regularly in person for worship or in furtherance of or to practise their beliefs'.[9] The criterion that it would need to be a 'manifestation of an individual's religion or beliefs to have a wedding officiated at by an officiant nominated by that organization'[10] would also rule out not only 'joke' organizations but also ones where there is no link between the beliefs held and the wedding.

But such limits can themselves be seen as respecting beliefs. Among our interviewees, Orla had registered the friend who was to conduct their non-legally binding ceremony "as a minister in the Pastafarian Church", but emphasized that this was "as a joke". In *De Wilde v The Netherlands*,[11] the European Court of Human Rights did not consider Pastafarianism to be a religion or belief within the meaning of Article 9 of the European Convention on Human Rights, noting that its underlying purpose was to criticize established religions through parody. Such groups would therefore not qualify to nominate officiants.

In our view, respecting beliefs also means respecting a *lack* of formal beliefs. The options for those who do not subscribe to a recognized system of belief should be just as rich in ritual and meaning. Across our study, we had examples of individuals who held no formal beliefs but had chosen to have a religious or Humanist wedding. In the case of those choosing a religious wedding, this was often to reflect their cultural upbringing and identity, or the beliefs of their partner or family,[12] rather than simply unreflectingly following tradition.[13] Where such considerations apply, individuals are likely to continue to choose to have a religious wedding regardless of what other options are available, even if it does not align with their personal beliefs. In the case of Humanist weddings, some individuals commented that their values aligned with Humanism even where they did not define themselves as Humanist; such individuals are similarly likely to continue to choose to have a Humanist wedding regardless of what other options are available. But we also had examples of individuals who struggled to label themselves as holding particular beliefs and who found that a ceremony

---

[9]   Law Commission (2022) *Celebrating Marriage: A New Weddings Law* (19 July), para 4.256.
[10] Law Commission (2022), para 2.43.
[11] App no 9476/19.
[12] See Chapter 5.
[13] See Chapter 5 on the way in which individuals actively negotiated the form of their ceremonies.

led by an independent celebrant or by a friend or family member enabled them to have rituals that reflected the importance they attached to the commitment they were making without having to articulate formal beliefs that they did not hold.

Changing the law as to where weddings can be held, who can officiate at them, and what form the ceremony can take would go a long way to enable couples to marry in accordance with their formalized or unformalized beliefs. But respecting beliefs also means respecting the views of different belief organizations as to whether a marriage can take place between two persons of the same sex, or who hold different beliefs. Under the Law Commission's scheme, religious officiants would be able to refuse to officiate at same-sex weddings and would continue to be specifically protected from any potential claim under the Equality Act 2010 on account of that refusal. As a result, the choices available to same-sex couples or couples with different beliefs is likely to continue to be limited. That said, different views may exist within any given religious tradition. Within our study, we had Christian, Jewish, and Muslim individuals who conducted same-sex weddings. Under the Law Commission's scheme any religious group that meets the criteria for a nominating organization would be able to opt in to conduct same-sex weddings.

At an individual level, a common view among those conducting ceremonies was that making a vow in accordance with one's beliefs or values supported commitment. Thus, one imam, Ahmed, spoke of the "deeper meaning" of the *nikah*: "When you've got something sealed as a contract ... you take more of a responsibility"; Pranab, a Hindu priest, spoke of a Hindu marriage as "a union of mind, body, and spirit"; and Tom, an Evangelical Christian minister, highlighted how the Christian ceremony included a "direct invitation that God will be at the centre of their relationship".

Interviewees similarly identified how making a vow that aligned with their beliefs made them feel more 'bound' to each other than they had in their civil wedding. Murron was particularly eloquent on this point:

'saying the vows in that circle in that instant made me think this is my religion and I'm pledging myself to this man in this way ... this is it. I can't break this. You have to mean what you're saying. Whereas when we were in the registry office, I know that's the legal part, but it didn't have so much meaning behind it.'

Our point here is not that commitment should have to be expressed in terms of a specific belief system. Indeed, many of the independent celebrants made similar points about the importance of couples being able to express their commitment to each other in words of their own choosing. As Bethany put it, that is what "makes it meaningful for them and hopefully that gives them the cement that's going to keep them together". Our point is rather that enabling individuals to express their legal commitment in accordance with their beliefs or values changes the nature of the ceremony for them. They are no longer simply repeating words that they have been told to say and which may have no intrinsic meaning for them.

Conclusion

We end as we began, with the Anglican wedding conducted while COVID-19 restrictions were still in force. Two of the older guests, listening to the service, assumed that the service was a specially truncated version, since it did not include many of the phrases with which they were familiar. But the service was in fact simply that prescribed in *Common Worship*, rather than the older liturgies with which they were more familiar.

As this illustrates, our expectations of what a wedding should include will inevitably be coloured by our experience of those we have attended. It can be hard to step outside one's own tradition to see what is distinctive about it and what may seem alien and alienating to those who do not share that tradition. Equally, perceptions of the same ritual may differ depending on the perspective of the individuals involved. Our study has shown, for example, how handfasting may have religious, spiritual, or cultural meanings to different people. As Wendy Leeds-Hurwitz has noted, '[i]f every wedding you attend incorporates the same symbols, it is possible to forget that ritual is a human construction, designed by people like yourself'.[14] For symbols and ritual, one could also read 'requirements' and 'law'.

Throughout this book, we have sought to showcase how individuals are choosing to be married in England and Wales today, not only to demonstrate the limitations of the current law but also to show just how beautiful, heartfelt, and meaningful these ceremonies are. With no substantial reform to weddings law since the 19th century, the gap between social and legal understandings of what makes a couple married has significantly widened. While more couples are choosing to cohabit without formalizing their relationship, marriage is still important for many, and many more than the official statistics suggest. Marriage law urgently needs to catch up and recognize the diversity of beliefs in England and Wales in the 21st century. Reform is needed both for the growing number of people who hold beliefs for which weddings law does not make adequate provision and for those

---

[14] Wendy Leeds-Hurwitz (2002) *Wedding as Text: Communicating Cultural Identities through Ritual* (Lawrence Erlbaum Associates), 94.

who have faith or spirituality but do not subscribe to a formal belief system. The Law Commission's recommendations for reform, if implemented, will provide a radical overhaul of an outdated system, thereby helping more couples celebrate their wedding in a manner which is reflective of the way they live and their beliefs in marriage.

Pseudonyms and Numbers Representing Study Participants

The table sets out the pseudonyms given to participants in the Nuffield Foundation-funded project in this book and the corresponding numbers used in our previous reports.

Aashvi	054	Atif	020
Abir	036	Ayman	D-131
Ada	012	Barbara	G-171
Adam	L-221	Benji	074
Adnan	080	Bethany	F-162
Ahmed	B-115	Carla	I-193
Aidan	059	Chloe	015
Ajey	055	Christine	H-183
Alice	024	Crystal	045
Amal	040	Cyrus	008
Amanda	022	Daisy	030
Amber	046	Damal	D-144
Amina	056	Dan	O-251
Andy	G-176	Dania	028
Anna	068	Darain	048
Anya	F-167	David	047
Arif	D-137	Dawn	G-174
Arjun	J-201	Deborah	F-163
Arun	043	Dev	J-202

Dharval	081	Mairead	062
Eda	037	Manizeh	005
Ellis	072B	Margaret	G-177
Emma	072A	Mary	016
Farah	061	Maryam	035
Farid	064	May	004A
Fariha	083A	Meera	071
Faye	039	Mel	H-185
Felix	083B	Miriam	006
Finn	N-241	Murron	010
Gaia	G-172	Musa	D-142
Grainne	032	Nadia	013
Gwydion	N-242	Orla	052
Haris	019	Parmita	079
Hazel	004B	Peter	075
Helen	076	Phoebe	027
Idrees	A-104	Polly	026
Ismail	C-123	Pranab	K-215
Jacob	I-192	Priya	042
Jamal	B-113	Rachael	L-225
Jan	H-181	Rahil	K-212
Jane	007	Rhoda	063
Jannat	058	Richard	L-222
Jasmine	060A	Rob	H-184
Jay	060B	Rupal	K-211
John	O-252	Ruth	F-164
Joyce	G-175	Salim	003
Karen	025	Sam	041
Karim	014	Samir	D-143
Kester	I-194	Sarah	049
Khalil	C-122	Satnam	P-261
Kiran	029	Shelley	G-173
Laila	021	Shikhar	J-203
Lakshmi	F-161	Simon	E-152
Laura	H-182	Simrat	009
Linda	073	Sita	067
Lucy	023	Sophea	M-232

Stella	078	Uzair	B-111
Sue	H-187	Vicky	044
Tara	M-231	Vikram	070
Tashi	F-165	Xayd	D-138
Tom	L-224	Yousha	D-134
Uma	066	Zahra	057

Index

References to footnotes show both the page number and the note number (13n2).

www.ingramcontent.com/pod-product-compliance
Lightning Source LLC
Chambersburg PA
CBHW070935030426
42336CB00014BA/2693